IMAGINAL LANDSCAPES

reflections on the mystical visions of
Jorge Luis Borges and Emanuel Swedenborg

IMAGINAL LANDSCAPES

reflections on the mystical visions of
Jorge Luis Borges and Emanuel Swedenborg

William Rowlandson

The Swedenborg Society
Swedenborg House
20-21 Bloomsbury Way
London WC1A 2TH

2015

To My Family

Published by:
The Swedenborg Society
Swedenborg House
20-21 Bloomsbury Way
London WC1A 2TH

Imaginal Landscapes © 2015, William Rowlandson / The Swedenborg Society
Foreword © 2015, Gary Lachman / The Swedenborg Society

Typeset at Swedenborg House.
Printed by T J International.
Book design/typeface: Stephen McNeilly

ISBN 978-0-85448-183-5
British Library Cataloguing-in-Publication Data.
A catalogue record for this book is available
from the British Library.

We have dreamt the world. We have dreamt it resistant, mysterious, visible, ubiquitous in space and firm in time; but we have left in its architecture tenuous and eternal interstices of unreason, so that we know it is false.

—Jorge Luis Borges

Foreword

Gary Lachman

In Buenos Aires in 1928 a young Jorge Luis Borges, the great Argentine poet and short story writer, had a mystical experience. Strolling through the northern ends of the city, he came upon a forlorn *barrio*, the kind of urban landscape he so often returns to in his stories. But, as William Rowlandson points out in this engaging essay, the scene held something more for Borges than the usual poetic charm. Something in the air that night reached Borges and for a moment he was transformed. From being a twenty-something poet enjoying a suggestive atmosphere that he knew well, Borges became something *more*. We don't, in fact, know exactly how long Borges's experience lasted, and in the context of its significance to ask 'how long' it did seems, as should soon become clear, oxymoronic. Because for at least a moment or two—alas, our limited vocabulary compels me to express it in this way—Borges entered eternity. He stepped out of time. He was no longer looking upon a fairly average neighbourhood on a fairly average night, but was hovering above it as it was some thirty years earlier, in the 1890s. As he wrote in his account of this experience, 'Feeling in Death', Borges felt he had become an 'abstract observer of the world', and that he had been given 'possession of the reticent or absent meaning of the word *eternity*'.

GARY LACHMAN

The actual feeling of being transported to another time—or indeed of being above time itself, and seeing it below one as a kind of vast landscape—was sufficiently powerful to remain with Borges for the rest of his life, but he was granted another insight that night as well. It was the recognition that, as Rowlandson writes, words can 'really mean what they mean'. 'Ecstasy', Rowlandson tells us, 'is not merely an intriguing word, it is real', something Borges discovered that evening about the word *eternity*. Although I am familiar with the uncanny experience of words 'suddenly meaning what they mean', I would turn this insight around. Words, I believe, always mean what they mean; it is we who do not always grasp their meaning, their true significance. The fault is not in words, in language, but in our limp grip on the meanings they convey, our tendency to relax our hold on reality—our consciousness, that is—and to take it for granted. All our art, poetry, literature and philosophy are attempts, frequently but not always successful, at reminding us that reality is real; they are a kind of wake-up call to what is. Borges knew full well what 'eternity' meant before finding himself in that suburban *barrio*, but for some reason that evening he *really* knew it. Eternity was not just a word or a vague notion of a 'long time'. It was real and immanent and all around him. He was in it and had been all his life. Borges, like most of us, had forgotten this, but something that evening reminded him. If we could grasp the mechanism involved in this 'remembering'—if we could, as it were, tie a string around our consciousness so as not to forget—we would, like Borges, be transformed.

Was Borges's experience mystical? That depends, of course, on your notion of what 'mystical' or 'mystic' means, and much of Rowlandson's essay is devoted to exploring this difficult question. I recognize the difficulty in pinning the meaning of mystical down: as St Augustine said about time, 'If you do not ask what it is, I know', and the same can be said of the mystical. But this is also true of those other fundamental elements of our experience. As with art, truth, love, life, reality, beauty, the meaning of mystical is at once self-evident and ambiguous. It is too basic to be expressed explicitly and too large to be held within secure limits. Only our mundane necessities can be expressed with utilitarian precision; the truly meaningful things are open-ended. This does not mean that the mystical is categorically ineffable, as many mystics have said. Like these other imponderables, it occupies the frontiers of our means of expression. It certainly stretches the limits of language to try to define 'mystic' or to express the meaning of a mystical experience; as the literary philosopher George Steiner remarked, our dictionaries lag behind our needs. But the vacant entries can be filled over time——at least I believe this is what my job as a writer is——and as Rowlandson points out, a consideration of language itself can be a trigger to the mystical. Perhaps only what is unsayable is worth saying, but then Wittgenstein already said that.

Borges, we know, was interested in mysticism and mystics, and one of the mystics who intrigued him was Swedenborg. Borges had no hesitation in calling Swedenborg a mystic; such a designation, he wrote, was 'extremely accurate'. Yet Borges also pointed out that Swedenborg did not meet the usual, often erroneous, expectations associated with the term. He was not an introverted lone nutter, secluding himself from others to contemplate his navel, but a profoundly social and practical man, characteristics that Borges, in an essay on Swedenborg, emphasized. Swedenborg too faced the difficulty of remembering and expressing what the angels told him on his visits to heaven and hell that so delighted Borges. Angelic speech, Swedenborg said, is unlike human language. Angels can say more in a minute than we can in an hour and can express in a few words more than we can in a book. A single angelic word can say more than I am trying to in this preface—a perhaps not too difficult task but the reader, I think, gets the gist of what Swedenborg means. Yet Swedenborg did not throw his quill pen down in despair. On the contrary, in a sometimes pedantic prose he patiently translated his angelic encounters into a kind of *Rough Guide* to inner worlds, recounting the kinds of fantastic voyages and impossible journeys that Borges loved.

GARY LACHMAN

'To be interested in mysticism is to be prepared to accept the possibility that what we are taught about time, space, life and death, is not necessarily the whole picture', Rowlandson writes. This is true. The following pages offer some ways in which our incomplete picture can be better filled in and may even suggest to some readers that they too are mystics, even if they didn't know.

London February 2014

IMAGINAL LANDSCAPES

reflections on the mystical visions of
Jorge Luis Borges and Emanuel Swedenborg

I felt as the dead feel. (Borges)

Borges, like Blake, walked the city streets. One evening in 1928, while he *wandered through each chartered street* of the northern margins of Buenos Aires, he fell outside time. The strange episode was to have such an effect on him that he published its brief account in his forthcoming book *The Language of the Argentines*, and republished the passage, verbatim, in two further works. He also referred to the matter in interviews in his later years.

In the account, which he entitled 'Feeling in Death', Borges writes that he set out that afternoon on a purposely purposeless walk, accomplishing 'to the unsatisfactory degree to which it is possible, what is called strolling at random'. Yet a certain 'gravitation' drew him towards the type of dusty, flyblown *barrio* that we find so often in his tales and poems. He meditated at a lonely street corner, 'taking in the night, in perfect, serene respite from thought'. The scene before him, timeless already in its poetic poverty, suddenly appeared to him not of the present moment, but of thirty years before:

> The glib thought *I am in the year eighteen hundred and something* ceased to be a few approximate words and deepened into reality. I felt as the dead feel, I felt myself to be an abstract observer of the world; an indefinite fear imbued with knowledge that is the greater clarity of metaphysics. No, I did not believe I had made my way upstream on the presumptive waters

of Time. Rather, I suspected myself to be in possession of the reticent or absent meaning of the inconceivable word *eternity*.

Borges was in his twenties, and so the experience was not a Proustian remembrance of childhood, but an instantaneous appearance in the unlived past. The experience, which he later referred to as one of the two mystical experiences of his life, plunged him deeply into philosophical questions of time—questions which dominated his work. Yet I feel that what was of even greater significance here was this sense that words can, suddenly, really mean what they mean. Ecstasy is not merely an intriguing word, it is real. The abstract word eternity is suddenly no longer abstract; it can, however fleetingly, be felt.

I have paid a lot of attention to this brief text, and have tried to imagine the afternoon's walk, the low houses and empty streets leading out onto the wide dusty plain; and I have tried to meditate upon this peaceful—if a little frightening—moment of timelessness. Whilst I have not found myself as present in that landscape as Borges clearly was in his vision, my focus returns to his focus on the meaningfulness of language. Borges, I sense, was astonished to understand that the accounts of ecstasy he had read in mystical texts not only described states which were real, but which he also could experience. 'Interstices of unreason' in the architecture of the world *do* occur, and they are astonishing, alarming, and marvellous; they are not mere poetic fancy. Reality is not stable, but stable enough for moments of utter strangeness to occur only very rarely.

One need never abandon the intellect, nor place faith over experience, nor adhere to a particular creed, nor be credulous or naïve, to recognize and experience the strange and the numinous.

He had not yet published those tales of the 1940s—*Ficciones* and *The Aleph*—which would propel him to international acclaim and which would engender the term 'Borgesian' (*borgeano*, in Spanish). Tales presenting, for example: a magician who dreams his son into existence; a man with perfect memory; a world existing in an encyclopaedia which begins to infect our world; the universe as an infinite library; the universe condensed into a tiny spot on a basement staircase; a coin that is all coins; a man granted by God a year of frozen time; an immortal who, weary of many centuries of existence, seeks mortality; and so on. Nor had he published those tales of the 1970s: a love affair in modern York that becomes a Viking saga; an infinite book; a one-sided disc. Yet all these later tales embody something of that uncanny quality of 'Feeling in Death'.

I see this moment as a vent from which energy and ideas hissed and bubbled throughout his life into the waters of his creative imagination.

Yes, his later fiction bears something of the flavour of 'Feeling in Death', but so does his poetry from before the account. In 1923 he had published the poems of *Fervour of Buenos Aires*, in which the young man contemplates lonely streets, buildings, statues and cemeteries, and recognizes the mythic, poetic nature of the city. Borges urges the reader to see that we perceive the world—its history, culture and geography—through myth, poetry and language. Reality is textual and text is reality. 'Feeling in Death' was thus an invocation—a spell cast by his poetic imagination; and the awe of the moment arrived with the understanding that his words had 'deepened into reality'. The episode inspired and was inspired by imagination. On this extraordinary night he had not transcended text, but entered ever deeper into text, into his own poetry. Language is magical. Reality is infused with psyche. Reality is poetic.

When in his eighties he visited Japan with his companion María Kodama, Borges was enchanted by the spiritual atmosphere of the Zen Buddhist and Shinto monasteries, and was keen to spend some months in retreat. He dialogued with a Zen monk, eager to correlate their more permanent spiritual state with his own fleeting states from his youth. That he published 'Feeling in Death' in three different works, that he discussed it in interviews in his seventies and eighties, and that he held the account in his mind whilst sitting, blind and enraptured, in a monastery, shows the prominence of the episode in his personal mythology.

WILLIAM ROWLANDSON

*

For the last twenty-five years of his studious life, the eminent philosopher and man of science Emanuel Swedenborg (1688-1772) resided in London. But as the English are not very talkative, he fell into the habit of conversing with devils and angels. (Borges)

Borges read Swedenborg with great devotion, and died with the project still unrealized of writing a book about his otherworld journeys. He paid close attention to Swedenborg's accounts of heavens and hells, the angelic and demonic beings encountered there, and his communication with the discarnate dead. Borges often suggested that he would like to be remembered as a reader more than as a writer; and in particular as a friend who happily recommends to others a book, poem or author. Just as I thank Borges for introducing me to Emanuel Swedenborg, so Borges thanked the nineteenth-century American poet Ralph Waldo Emerson.

Emerson lectured on Swedenborg and published a chapter entitled 'Swedenborg; or, The Mystic' in *Representative Men*, a book which Borges translated into Spanish. Emerson also depicted his own mystical experiences, most famously, in his essay *Nature*, where he describes an ecstatic state of consciousness:

> My head bathed by the blithe air, and uplifted into infinite spaces,—all mean egotism vanishes. I become a transparent eye-ball; I am nothing; I see all; the currents of the Universal Being circulate through me; I am part or particle of God.

There is thus a level of experience that Emerson was able to draw upon when considering Swedenborg and mysticism. Likewise, the psychologist and scholar of religion, William James, often inspired by his godfather Emerson, correlated accounts of mystics with his own mystical states (in part induced by nitrous oxide and ether) in formulating his chapter on mysticism in his mighty work *The Varieties of Religious Experience*. Borges inherited a fondness for William James from his father and their friend, a maverick philosopher called Macedonio Fernández (who communicated with James), and references to James are scattered amongst his work. He even explained how James inspired his own interpretation of mysticism. Whilst Emerson criticized Swedenborg's works as much as he praised them, and whilst James may have avoided too much discussion of Swedenborg in *Varieties* in order to distance himself from his father and godfather, nevertheless I feel that there is an integral relationship between their own anomalous—or mystical—experiences, and their reading of Swedenborg and their understanding of mysticism in general.

In the style of Emerson, Borges delivered lectures on Swedenborg which he later published, in which he called Swedenborg 'a mystic far more complex than the others'. Emerson's and Borges's accounts are fascinating, revealing much about their authors through their relationship with Swedenborg. They have much in common. Emerson writes that Swedenborg laboured 'with the heart and strength of the rudest Viking that his rough Sweden ever sent to battle'. Borges writes: 'No one was less like a monk than that sanguine Scandinavian who went much farther than Erik the Red'. They both also published similar stirring poems to Swedenborg.

Borges saw a profound reality in the voyages of Swedenborg, something worthy of close attention. Whilst his own experience, so carefully recorded in 'Feeling in Death', clearly gave him a sensation of something valuable, some feeling about the flexibility of our relationship with time, some sense of the numinous, Borges seemed to see in Swedenborg a slow, measured, open and scientific exploration of this space. Swedenborg appeared to inhabit this strange landscape.

It seems that Borges was amazed to find in Swedenborg someone who did not find this state of vision ineffable, but who instead was capable of producing from it prosaic and astonishingly detailed volumes in Latin.

A Viking indeed: strong, adventuresome, brave. Yet also a son of the Enlightenment: observant, meticulous and unswayed by the constraints of faith. 'That's to say', says Borges, 'he was an eminently *practical* man'.

Why this insistence upon Swedenborg's sanity, upon his rigorous method, and upon his immense body of work on mineralogy, engineering, anatomy, astronomy, economics and mathematics? I feel that Borges is indicating to us that Swedenborg can be trusted, that he is a reliable guide through this otherworld reality. But what is this extraordinary reality depicted by Swedenborg? What distant shores did this valiant Viking explore? What was his mystical vision?

By saying that Emerson's eyeball experience, James's variety of experiences, and Borges's state of timelessness were all mystical, I have already made assumptions both about the experiences and about the meaning of the word mystical. However, despite the currency of the term, there is little consensus about what mystic, mystical or mysticism mean. What is an anomalous experience? What is a mystical experience? Is a mystic simply someone who has had a mystical experience, someone who regularly has a mystical experience, or someone who lives a mystical experience? When Emerson labelled Swedenborg a mystic, what did he mean? Was Emerson himself a mystic? Was James? Was Borges? Am I? Are you? What on earth do these questions mean?

*

The mystic is the person who has realized that the game is a game. (Alan Watts)

Assuming, of course, that it is important to do so, how does one go about answering such questions? What earns someone the title mystic? Is there a commonality to mystics' experiences, to their accounts, to their lives?

Read the mystics, one might answer, what do they say? Yet there is no easily defined school of mystics. There are many writers of many texts from many traditions, cultures and times, who have been called, by someone, at some time, mystics. Or their texts have been called mystical. Or not. Fascinatingly, there is a long debate concerning whether Emerson was or was not a mystic. He was a secular mystic, not a Christian mystic. He was an agnostic mystic—a term that has been used to describe Borges. He was a 'Nature Mystic'. He was, and this is a favourite of mine, a 'Yankee Mystic'.

Aldous Huxley, for example, had a profound mystical experience, which he recounts in *Doors of Perception*, and which he correlates according to mystical traditions, oriental and occidental, in *Heaven and Hell*. Others disagreed, and argued that Huxley was no mystic, as his experiences were induced through mescaline (and thereafter in increasingly heroic doses of LSD), and were therefore not really mystical.

How does one determine who is or is not a mystic unless there is some critical appraisal of their writings in general?

Well there is. There is the scholarship of mysticism, pioneered by William Inge, Dean of St Paul's Cathedral, and William James over a century ago. This scholarship reveals countless attempts to define mysticism by consulting prime texts, correlating the texts with other accounts, including perhaps the experiences of the scholar, and seeking the key characteristics. Yet consensus is not forthcoming in the scholarship—far from it. One fundamental problem is that the terms employed to define mysticism are themselves dazzlingly strange and vague. As such, when James suggests 'noetic' as one such criterion, we must assume a consensual understanding of this term. This may sound pedantic, but it is alarming how often one encounters a declaration that a certain poet-author-theologian was or was not a mystic because their experience was or was not 'unitive', 'extravertive' or 'ineffable'. These terms themselves are thorny.

A standard approach to defining mysticism is to set out what mysticism is not. Dean Inge decrees that 'I cannot accept any definition which identifies mysticism with excited or hysterical emotionalism, with sublimated eroticism, with visions and revelations, with supernatural (dualistically opposed to natural) activities'. William James suggests that the term is often thrown as reproach 'at any opinion which we regard as vague and vast and sentimental'. Evelyn Underhill argues:

> What then do we really mean by mysticism? A word which is impartially applied to the performances of mediums and the ecstasies of the saints, to 'menticulture' and sorcery, dreamy poetry and mediaeval art, to prayer and palmistry, the doctrinal excesses of Gnosticism, and the tepid speculations of the Cambridge Platonists—even, according to William James, to the higher branches of intoxication—soon ceases to have any useful meaning.

W K Fleming follows this line: 'mysticism has nothing whatever to do with occult pursuits, magic and the like'. R C Zaehner, likewise, was keen to separate the mystical experience from experiences of paranormal, the occult, intoxication or even non-religious experiences. Walter Stace writes that 'The word "mysticism" is popularly used in a variety of loose and inaccurate ways. Sometimes anything is called "mystical" which is misty, foggy, vague, or sloppy. [...] There is nothing misty, foggy, vague, or sloppy about mysticism'. Neither, he thunders, is it any form of 'mystery-mongering [...] hocus-pocus [...] or the occult'. Nor 'anything to do with spiritualism, or ghosts, or table-turning'. Nor 'what are commonly called parapsychological phenomena such as telepathy, telekinesis, clairvoyance, precognition. These are not mystical phenomena...'

A more recent approach to mysticism, such as *Varieties of Anomalous Experience*, separates mystical experience from the other chapter topics: Hallucinatory Experiences; Synaesthesia; Lucid Dreaming; Out-of-Body Experiences; Psi-related Experiences; Alien Abduction Experiences; Past-Life Experiences; Near-Death Experiences; and Anomalous Healing Experiences. In so doing, the kinship and the distinction between these experiences are illustrated.

I would ask, though, whether these other matters are not themselves characteristic of mysticism. The case of Swedenborg is a pertinent example. Not one of the many biographies of Swedenborg fails to emphasize his tremendous psychic abilities, such as his helping a countess to locate a missing receipt after speaking to her deceased husband, or his relaying a secret to the queen of Sweden that only her dead brother could have known. Immanuel Kant, after all, only read Swedenborg's works because of the legend of his clairvoyant vision of the fire in Stockholm whilst he was dining in Gothenburg, one of his 'minor miracles' (to use Wilson Van Dusen's expression). It may even be suggested that Swedenborg's enduring reputation lies not so much with his voluminous biblical exegesis, nor even with his accounts of heavens and hells, but with these well-documented psychic abilities.

Sir Arthur Conan Doyle, for example, dismisses in one paragraph the entire theological dimension of Swedenborg's works, 'and his tiresome exegesis of the Scriptures', and focuses exclusively on the prophetic visions and 'psychic powers', seeing them as foundational in the history of Spiritualism.

Even Jung, who read Swedenborg in his university days with great sympathy, appeared little concerned with Swedenborg's theological ethos and far more so with his 'psychic phenomena', such as 'Swedenborg's well-attested vision of the great fire in Stockholm'.

Something encourages people to read Swedenborg, and the hooks that often arrest attention and which seem to give validity to his accounts of angels, demons, heavens and hells are, precisely, these miraculous abilities. Why accept one miracle and not another?

William James, meanwhile, placed 'passivity' as one of the defining characteristics of the mystical experience. He recognized 'preliminary voluntary operations, as by fixing the attention, or going through certain bodily performances'; and as such, Swedenborg's exercises of breath control and meditation (comparable to those in yogic practices) are accommodated. Yet James explained that 'when the characteristic sort of consciousness once has set in, the mystic feels as if his own free will were in abeyance'. Swedenborg, however, seems a most active participant in his experiences, fully able to reflect, act and decide.

As detailed in his *Spiritual Diary*, Swedenborg was also a dreamer of profound lucidity, engaging in long dialogues with the characters encountered in the dreamworld. Yet a lucid dreamer is not necessarily a mystic, nor is a mystic necessarily a lucid dreamer.

It is thus no simple matter to separate Swedenborg's lucid dreaming, clairvoyance and mediumship from his mystical nature. In many accounts, they *are* his mystical nature.

Indeed, most of the features of anomalous experiences that Stace would so firmly assert do not constitute the mystical—communication with the dead, telepathy, clairvoyance, precognition, ecstasy—are as pertinent to Swedenborg as they are to many other mystics appraised in the scholarship.

Borges, true to his trickster form, muddies the waters by making many forthright claims about mystics and non-mystics, stating, for example, that Plotinus, Silesius, Swedenborg, Blake and his friend Xul Solar were all *místicos*, whilst Pascal, Teresa de Ávila, Juan de la Cruz and Luis de León were not. Upon what basis did he make those claims? Most likely his dismissal was not an evaluation of their supposed mystical attributes, but derived from his readiness to mock sacred cows, upset Catholic traditionalists, and choose his cultural heroes from the northern climes. Thus his love for Swedenborg cannot be separated from his love of Viking legends, Icelandic sagas, Anglo-Saxon poetry and his own Northumbrian ancestry. He contrasted Swedenborg both with those mystics one may consider 'removed from the circumstances and urgencies we call [...] reality', and those characterized by 'the ecstasy of a rapt and fainting soul'. As such, in his few comments about St Teresa and 'the Spaniards', one may suggest that Borges judged her to be pious, orthodox, ecstatic, and removed from worldly concerns. I am not certain this is accurate, as whilst she may have been both pious and ecstatic, one cannot judge Teresa to be docile and obedient to church authority, nor anything other than deeply involved in the political ecclesiastical machinations of her time. In fact, I feel that had Borges reflected on how deftly Teresa deflected Inquisitorial attention, and how rebellious she was, he may have been more willing to call her a mystic.

Dante was not a mystic, Borges maintains, because his vision was self-willed rather than spontaneous and unbidden. In this sense Borges would appear to concur with James's position that mystical states are passive. Dante was not a visionary because of the length of this vision, which, Borges argues, would be unsustainable. In this sense we see James's category of 'transient'. The vision itself was inspired by poetic faith, and was therefore culturally conditioned within established theological and artistic frameworks. Furthermore, Dante wrote in verse, and there is no possible way that he could have experienced the various circles of the *Divine Comedy* in such an aesthetic language.

These are strange judgements. Had Swedenborg written in verse, would he therefore not have been a mystic? Surely all language, whatever the style, is an approximation of the experience? Did Swedenborg experience his heavens and hells in Latin? Borges's criteria for judging mysticism are thus far from straightforward.

Stace argued that the word mystic 'always mean[s] a person who himself has had mystical experience'. Fine, but what is a mystical experience? And is a 'mystical' text necessarily the account of a mystical experience, or the product of a mystic? Can a mystical account be invented? If so, is it still mystical? What of a parody? There is a passage in the tale 'The Aleph' in which Borges the narrator undergoes a profound mystical experience, perceiving the entirety of the universe in a tiny fragment of space-time. It is a miraculous account.

But it is a useless ecstasy, as the impossible Aleph serves the narrator only as a means of prying into the private correspondence of his former lover and her cousin, and serves its owner, Daneri, only as material for pretentious poetry. It is ridiculous.

Borges's close friend, Estela Canto, wrote a review of 'The Aleph', calling it a 'tale of a mystical experience'. Borges was delighted with the review, and thanked Canto for being the only critic to perceive the tale's mystical quality.

But is it really mystical?

Probably not, as it is a carefully crafted simulacrum of a mystical experience. It is a fiction.

But then what of 'Feeling in Death'? There is a fictional feel to that text. What of Boehme, Meister Eckhart, St Teresa, Swedenborg, Blake? All we have is text; and what, really, does fiction mean? Surely the mystical qualities of a text lie not so much with the perceived mystical abilities of the author, but with the relationship between text and reader?

I had taken 'The Aleph' to be something of a joke. I then understood that as a joke it is no less magical. It pulls you in, demands your critical attention, makes you look around and question what you are reading. It is funny. Is *that* mystical?

Two characters—the ridiculous Daneri and the forlorn, love-struck narrator—both experience the plenitude of the universe in a spot on a basement step that is later destroyed. The readers are invited to consider what *they* would do if presented with this? Would they produce poetry any better that Daneri's? Why should such ecstasy not occur in so mundane a location? Why should the reader not be enraptured, even knowing the tale's fictionality?

I then reread 'The God's Script'—a remarkable tale that I had read as another pastiche of a mystical state. Tzinacán, an Aztec priest dying in a dungeon following Cortés's conquest, having witnessed the destruction of the pyramids, and having resisted revealing secret treasure to the Spaniards, dedicates his days to locating and deciphering the words of God, written during Creation in Creation itself. His cell neighbour is a jaguar, whose stripes and spots he begins to interpret, culminating in an ecstatic revelation in which he reads and understands God's writing.

But he refuses to divulge it to the reader.

We are left where we began, searching. But now we have another companion

—the Aztec priest. He experienced dissolution in the universe, unity, loss of selfhood. He felt himself part of the godhead, yet can only describe it to us through words—words which fail to capture the experience. These are mystical words. Pastiche or not, exquisite artifice or faithful testimonial, it is a *real* account because it *is* an account.

'The God's Script' is an astonishing tale. It is written by the Aztec priest. It is written by Borges. It is a dialogue between Borges and the priest, transcribed by Borges. It is written by Borges the Aztec priest. It is about Borges. It is about the reader. It is about the reader the Aztec Priest. It is a dazzling tale of a profound spiritual journey. It is a hero's journey.

'I have felt my tales so deeply', wrote Borges, 'that I have told them, well, using strange symbols so that people might not find out that they were all more or less autobiographical. The stories were about myself, my personal experiences'.

And so many other tales share this sense of revelation and oblivion. In a later tale called 'Undr' from *The Book of Sand*, a man is told at the beginning of his life's wanderings that only he can find his secret word—indeed the search is the word. But the secret word cannot be revealed.

There is a tiny tale snuck away amidst the poems of *In Praise of Darkness* called 'The Ethnographer' ('The Anthropologist' in other translations). A young man, Fred Murdock, is urged by his professor to go on field research with a tribe of Native Americans in order to gather material for his dissertation. In particular he is urged to discover 'the secret that the *brujos* reveal to the initiates'. Over the months living on the prairie, Murdock is utterly transformed, learns to perceive reality in a different language, and learns to dream and recount his dreams to his *maestro*. His true initiation arrives when he dreams of the bison. He has undergone a radical shift in his relationship with reality, centred on a dream encounter with a totem animal.

Much to the chagrin of his professor, he never writes his thesis, and never reveals the secret of the *brujos*. 'Now that I have the secret, I could explain it in a hundred different and even contradictory ways'. And yet, he continues, 'The secret, I should tell you, is not as valuable as the steps that brought me to it. Those steps have to be taken, not told'.

What, therefore, does Murdock learn out in the wilderness? Well, in order to answer that we need to head out to the wilderness ourselves. Only then might Murdock's experience be understood. We must become Murdock—the hero, the fool—and learn to listen to our dreams. Our mythic prairie may be within, and our medicine man may be the memory of a grandfather or a character from a book. What totem animal might appear?

So many of Borges's tales are such journeys of discovery, focused on something revealed yet unrevealed, experienced yet incommunicable. Yet Borges, mercurial, trickster, never lets the reader relax into bliss. Traps are laid in the path. Like a Zen master he answers your questions with a slap to the head. Pay attention. Nothing is quite what it seems. Make no glib assumptions. All tales are self-referential, self-mocking. They are snakes swallowing their own tails, their own tales. Thus a mystical text is not a mystical text as it is a parody of a mystical text but it still may be a mystical text. But anyway, what is a mystical text?

*

We pass into mystical states from out of ordinary consciousness as from a less into a more, as from a smallness into a vastness, and at the same time as from an unrest to a rest. (William James)

Perhaps the question about what mysticism is or is not is not answerable. But it is valuable, as it fuels the exploration. The word mysticism clearly means something, and so whilst too precise a meaning may discount experiences otherwise accommodated by the term, too loose a definition would allow any experience to muscle in under its banner, rendering the term meaningless. One solution is to combine together all the defining characteristics as put forward by over a century of scholars. This then becomes a wild and unwieldy shopping list riddled with contradictions, and the selection of one defining category over another becomes either arbitrary or an attempt to match the text with the theory. Another solution is to seek a general term, generous enough to embrace the various scholars' findings, yet limited enough to guarantee some purchase on the term.

The best I could imagine is 'mysticism is mysterious'. This is not particularly helpful.

There are baffling contradictions, confusions and conflations in the scholarship. From James's four definitions: *ineffable*, *noetic*, *transient* and *passive*, through Underhill's five stages, I was guided towards Andrew Rawlinson's influential model in which he charts mystics according to a graph of *hot*, *cool*, *structured* and *unstructured*. This odd but surprisingly comprehensible model then led me to an article by transpersonal psychologist Michael Daniels, 'Making Sense of Mysticism', in which he runs through the century of scholarship, incorporates Rawlinson, and sketches an eye-wateringly complex model with multiple taxonomical layers on horizontal and vertical axes.

The graph brought to my mind the Chinese encyclopaedia called *The Heavenly Emporium of Benevolent Knowledge* in Borges's 1942 essay 'The Analytical Language of John Wilkins'. This absurd taxonomy of animals, which so tickled Michel Foucault that he discussed it in the opening of *The Order of Things*, is worth reproducing here in its entirety:

> In its distant pages it is written that animals are divided into (a) those that belong to the emperor; (b) embalmed ones; (c) those that are trained; (d) suckling pigs; (e) mermaids; (f) fabulous ones; (g) stray dogs; (h) those that are included in this classification; (i) those that tremble as if they were mad; (j) innumerable ones; (k) those drawn with a very fine camel's-hair brush; (l) etcetera; (m) those that have just broken the flower vase; (n) those that at a distance resemble flies.

It occurred to me that there was something similarly absurd at the heart of the scholarship of mysticism, based upon the very strangeness of mysticism itself. Mystical texts are embalmed, fabulous, stray, tremble as if they were mad, etcetera... If, indeed, a mystical experience is ineffable, then inevitably all theoretical approaches to the experience are hindered by, precisely, its ineffability. Mysticism is that which is not ordinary, knowable, understandable, definable. If it were easily describable, then, I would venture, it would not be mystical.

By definition indefinable.

A more profound revelation then shook me: the scholarship of mysticism can be mystical.

At first I felt something exasperating in running through endless academic approaches to the deistic or the non-deistic, the extravertive or the intravertive, the hot or the cool, the perennialist or the essentialist, as I felt that these questions rarely confront actual and pressing ontological, existential questions. Perhaps the questions should not concern whether Emerson was a 'religious mystic' or a 'nature mystic', nor whether Swedenborg's experiences were 'hot' or 'cool', 'structured' or 'unstructured', but what are we, as readers, to do with their texts? How do the texts affect us? Blake (regardless of whether he was or was not a mystic) would surely have raged against so much academic fussiness.

Swedenborg, likewise, was critical of scholarly debates that served as mere displays of erudition rather than interrogating the nature of reality, as he demonstrates in *Heaven and Hell*:

> If people have loved the academic disciplines only in order to sound learned, without using them to develop their ability to reason, taking delight in their pride at the contents of their memories, they love sandy areas and prefer them to meadows and gardens because sandy areas correspond to these kinds of study. People who are wrapped up in knowing the doctrines of churches, their own and others', without applying them to life, love stony

areas and live among rock piles. They avoid cultivated land because it is repulsive to them.

Swedenborg would have been equally dismayed at seeing his moral theology ignored and his own status pinned to an entry on a graph.

But after meditating further on this strange scholarship, I came to see the stirring words employed by the scholars to declare and defend and define these states of consciousness as themselves mysterious, extraordinary and wonderful: *numinous*, *sacred*, *unitive*, *ineffable*, *transcendental*, *transpersonal*, *psychedelic*, *holotropic*, *timeless*... These words are not merely definitions of mysticism; they *are* mystical, poetic, inspiring. The scholars and the poets will know that these words are all approximations, yet they recognize that language is all we have.

The texts of the mystics and those of the scholars are maps. They are also guides.

As such, St Teresa writes in her autobiography of the ascent of the soul in four stages: 'mental prayer'; 'prayer of quiet'; 'devotion of union'; and 'devotion of ecstasy or rapture'. Evelyn Underhill writes of the five fundamental stages in the development of the mystical individual:

(1) The awakening of the Self to consciousness of Divine Reality. (2) Purgation (3) Illumination (4) 'mystic pain' or 'mystic death', the Purification of the Spirit or Dark Night of the Soul. (5) Union: the true goal of the mystic quest.

Both texts—the mystic's and the scholar's—offer the reader steps to follow on a spiritual journey. The mystic may be scholar, the scholar may be mystic.

Varieties of Religious Experience, likewise, is a work of great spiritual gravitas, guiding the reader along a path through 'other cases of sense of God's presence', happiness, evil, healthy-mindedness, and James's own autobiographical dark night entitled 'The Sick Soul'. It is a solemn and devotional volume.

Inge's words, written to clarify, thus become beautifully mysterious and religious. The language is liturgical, like a Latin mass, magical in its bewildering senselessness:

> The charge of 'pantheistic tendency' will not, I hope, be brought against me without due consideration. I have tried to show how the Johannine Logos-doctrine, which is the basis of Christian Mysticism, differs from Asiatic Pantheism, from Acosmism, and from (one kind of) evolutionary Idealism. Of course, speculative Mysticism is nearer to Pantheism than to Deism; but I think it is possible heartily to eschew Deism without falling into the opposite error.

And the full-page graph drawn up by Michael Daniels is not absurd and useless, it is absurd and fantastic. It is itself a sacred text, a mandala on x and y axes, a penetration into mystery, a map of hidden reality. Blake would not rage against any of the scholarship as long as it was creative, beautiful. And why should I not treat Daniels' model as beautiful: 'Hot, Warm, Cold—Thou, All, We, It, I—God(s) or Divine Being(s), Nature or Cosmos', etc., triangulated against 'Numinous, Dialogic, Synergic, Unitive, Nondual'. This is a magical text.

And so the debates, disputes and refutations that emerge—such as Underhill's aversion to James's intoxication, or Zaehner's disquiet at Huxley's use of terms properly suited to orthodox religious traditions—are not problems to be resolved but questions that propel us deeper into the unknown. The strange binaries that are drawn up: bidden or unbidden; induced or passive; one-off or repeatable; intravertive or extravertive; inward or outward; theistic or agnostic; perennialist or structuralist; hot or cool; structured or unstructured… all these oppositions create friction that impels us further into the mystery.

Where I had at first seen as exasperating the strange debates about strange words, I now understood that everyone was trying, somehow, to find words to describe *something*. And to explore these works is to allow these words to become part of one's vocabulary. They are baffling, but they might make some sense if one seeks their sense, permits their sense to be revealed. Words have been employed and debated because they are meaningful. And words are not owned—they can be meaningful to anyone.

So an exploration into mysticism can be mystical. And if it is not, then perhaps it is not a proper exploration.

*

O waves of probable / and improbable / Universes— / Everybody's right
(Allen Ginsberg—'Laughing Gas')

I thus came to understand that the debate which had interested me about mysticism and psychedelics was not a problem to be resolved, but was a discussion precisely about the meaningfulness of language and the relationship between words and experience.

Some authors were affronted that reverent language could be employed in what they saw to be an irreverent fashion. They were trying to protect these words from being kicked about willy-nilly. They were also arguing that mysticism is more than a flash-in-the-pan, more than a spectacle of *son et lumière*. The mystical trip lasts a lifetime, or longer.

Others were experiencing something catalysed by acid, mushrooms, laughing gas, mescaline or ayahuasca, and saying: 'but don't you see, the only language I can use is that which belongs to spiritual traditions: Buddhist, Hindu, Native American, Catholic, etc.—what other language can I use?' And they were saying: 'and I *am* set upon a mystical path—a journey of discovery—and these intense experiences are part of that journey, providing immeasurably valuable knowledge'.

Jung, as an old man, learned of Huxley's mescaline revelations, yet, knowing the depths and breadths of our souls, and knowing that this awesome vocabulary of the mystical and the religious was powerful and profoundly meaningful, he simply warned *be careful—be careful*—remember 'Der Zauberlehrling [Sorcerer's Apprentice], who learned from his master how to call the ghosts but did not know how to get rid of them again...' As if to corroborate Jung after his death, Marie-Louis von Franz, Jung's associate, wrote scathingly about the messianic complex and ego inflation that she perceived LSD to have produced in Tim Leary. Both she and Jung understood that mystical experience catalysed by psychedelics could shift the tectonics of the psyche with more force than some ecstatic trippers were prepared or able to accept.

It became clear to me that a debate about whether or not psychedelics could produce mystical experiences was really a debate about who owns the words. Each addition to the dialogue is a new story, a new platform for expression, another bend in the road onwards towards experience. What matters is not so much how one arrives at a particular state of consciousness, but how to proceed. Can these experiences be articulated, shared? Where do the explorations lead?

Stace was insistent that the word mystic should not be applied simply to 'anyone who is sympathetic to mysticism'. Why so insistent? How far can one judge mere sympathy? Is not sympathy the first step towards a mystical state of consciousness? Without sympathy one simply will not begin. Perhaps one risks psychosis, if there is the intuition of the experience without the sympathy. Any exploration of consciousness surely must proceed from the understanding that consciousness *can* be explored.

Profound engagement with the word mysticism can thus be mystical.

To be interested in mysticism is to accept that the term 'mysticism' is worthy of investigation and that something useful may be derived from this study. This implies taking seriously the claims made both by those known as mystics, and the conclusions drawn by scholars. One would therefore entertain the possibility that the texts of mystics—such as Swedenborg's accounts of conversations with angels and demons and his voyages to heaven and hell—are not the ramblings of the insane nor outright lies.

But if neither delusion nor lie—ah, what then!

Borges felt something on that lonely evening on the outskirts of Buenos Aires; something that he tried and, according to him, failed, to describe. Some feeling, emotion, knowledge or merely some presence was experienced. And, as I argued earlier when discussing Emerson and James, the scholar searches for a language to describe something experienced or intuited (the same thing, really), to discover the commonalities of experience—*their* experience perhaps—across time and culture. Some modality of human experience is described, is appraised and is debated. It was a personal relationship with the experience that drove these learned souls onwards, granting them what Jung would call *libido*, or psychic energy, urging them onwards in reading accounts, poring over the diverse literatures in search of means of describing *something* experienced. What, after all, provided Jung such energy to study antique alchemical texts (even whilst visiting India) if not some correlation with experience—his and his patients'?

Bertrand Russell, for example, wrote lengthy essays early and late in his life about mysticism. Both essays are compelling, arguing through faultless logic that the truth claims of mystics are absurd. I found his conclusions beautiful rather than dispiriting, as, following Borges, I take truth claims, in general, to be absurd. Russell dedicated energy and time to these essays and, even if dismissive, he must have been fascinated by the subject.

He later describes in his autobiography how, as a young man, he had experienced a sudden state of utter desolation in which he *felt* rather than *thought* 'the loneliness of the human soul'. 'Nothing', he reflected, 'can penetrate it except the highest intensity of the sort of love that religious teachers have preached'. This state remained with him for many years:

The mystic insight which I then imagined myself to possess has largely faded, and the habit of analysis has reasserted itself. But something of what I thought I saw in that moment has remained always with me, causing my attitude during the first war, my interest in children, my indifference to minor misfortunes and a certain emotional tone in all my human relations.

We can thus see his harsh critique of mysticism to be a scrutiny of himself—a mode of self-enquiry. We see, furthermore, that in that brief instant as a young man, he suddenly experienced the values that dominated the rest of his life: pacifism, activism, anticlericalism, and 'a desire almost as profound as that of the Buddha to find some philosophy which should make human life endurable'. This was, indeed, strong noetic medicine...

Every investigation is thus an intervention, every search a path.

To be interested in mysticism is, ultimately, to be open to mysticism.

To be interested in mysticism is thus to ask the question, 'What is mysticism?', and in so doing to enquire about one's own life, one's own states of consciousness, one's own relationship with reality, to ask: have any of my experiences been mystical? If so, what does that say about me? Can I be a mystic? What experiences am I capable of achieving? Where next?

To be interested in mysticism is to be prepared to accept the possibility that what we are taught about time, space, life and death, is not necessarily the whole picture.

To be interested in mysticism is to explore life's 'interstices of unreason'.

*

This circle was a temple, long ago devoured by fire, which the malarial jungle had profaned and whose god no longer received the homage of men.
(Borges)

It seems appropriate to me that I should concern myself with exploring this peculiar word mysticism, as I feel that such concerns are integrally related to a fascination I have maintained since childhood with the strange and the weird; from when I first felt the tingling fear of the dark, of ghost stories and of spooky woodlands in the winter dusk. I recall reading late into the nights Arthur C Clarke's *Mysterious World*, *World of Strange Powers* and *Chronicles of the Strange and Mysterious*, contemplating the photographs and drawings of lake monsters, Bigfoot, alien visitors, foo fighters and other UFOs, ghostly apparitions, the Nazca Lines, colossal stones, Victorian ectoplasm...

I was brought up on Salisbury Plain where daily dog walks led me to three long barrows. Magic is felt sitting, smoking, for hours on an ancestor's burial mound gazing over the chalk grassland.

Another barrow was deep in the artillery live-firing area. There is a sense of exhilaration I can still recapture of standing by the beech trees, gazing north beyond the red danger signs, then slipping quietly through the gorse, along the tank tracks, to the barrow, fenced off with barbed wire and no-digging signs. As with the mysterious valleys, tors and mossy woodlands of north-west Dartmoor, whose secrets have been sealed off by the army, there is something otherworldly in such a landscape. Such a feeling is reflected in W G Sebald's description of the decaying military landscape of Orfordness.

The wheat fields near the various white horses on the escarpments leading off the Plain then began to break out in strange circles and glyphs that still beguile me every summer. There is a blustery debate that intrigues me: are the crop formations made by aliens or are they 'fake'? How can they be fake? What is a fake crop formation? They are magnificent and mysterious—awesome and daimonic—regardless of who made them. They are mighty mandalas in a landscape that shimmers with ancient numinosity.

I felt something magical and otherworldly as a young child in the long colourful smoky procession of travellers' buses, vans and trucks as they trundled slowly down the A303 towards some festival site (before Thatcher's police smashed their homes and their community). To my young mind they were fairy folk beckoning me to flee with them...

As an eighteen-year-old I finally caught up with them, living for many weeks in and amidst trees sentenced for felling for a new road. On many occasions, a joyous confluence of music, fire, cider, mud, damp tobacco and the companionship of old trees produced a sense of wellbeing that blooms in my memory when I consider the peak experiences of my life.

My fascination with megalithic structures began early and grows insatiably, and I have travelled widely in Britain, Brittany, Portugal, Spain and Sardinia to visit alignments.

Huge stones, astronomically aligned, standing defiantly and mysteriously on the lonely moorland, hewn by ancient technologies in distant hills, raised for unknown gods. Colossal lumps of numinosity. Deep magic. Awesome 'interstices of unreason'.

I have crawled along the dark passages of burial chambers, sitting quietly in stone niches, protected by the ageless stone from the gusty rainy wind outside.

I have drummed for many years, and explore the dazzling inner landscapes presented by solitary and group rhythms. I evoke images from my childhood—a beech tree and a tunnel—to travel up up up and down down down, guided by the drum and rattle.

As I contemplate my contemplation of the word mysticism, it is clear to me that all of this is connected. There is a presence, a secret flavour, some subtle experience, some intrigue, some excitement, an alluring *something* that is present throughout all these accounts of the stranger scope of human capacity. It is a sense of the mysterious, of experiences that defy conventional explanation. It is a sense captured by evolutionary biologist J B S Haldane in a line so often repeated by Terence McKenna: 'My own suspicion is that the universe is not only queerer than we suppose, but queerer than we *can* suppose'.

It is a sense that permeates Swedenborg's *Heaven and Hell*.

A contemplation of mystery—in all its many forms—brings a sense of the numinous. The numinous, as both Otto and Jung would aver, is the vibrating heart of the sacred and the religious, and is thus experienced in moments of ritual, worship, ceremony, and meditation. Yet it is also sensed in moments of utter strangeness, such as divination, temporal anomalies, paraphenomena, synchronicity, or, in Jung's baroque expression, a 'so-called catalytic exteriorization phenomenon'. These experiences are revitalizing, giving some essence of Blake's 'Energy is Eternal Delight'.

Such experiences are mystical, I would argue, if they appear magical, if they inspire the awe of mystery, a sense of wonder, a respect for the mysterious.

*

A small child is taken to the zoo for the first time. This child may be any one of us, or to put it another way, we have been this child and have forgotten about it. In these grounds—these terrible grounds— the child sees living animals he has never before glimpsed; he sees jaguars, vultures, bison, and—what is still stranger—giraffes. [. . .] Let us pass now from the zoo of reality to the zoo of mythologies, to the zoo whose denizens are not lions but sphinxes and griffons and centaurs. (Borges)

I have considered mystery and mysticism in relation to the fabled imaginative skills of children. It may not be that children are so visionary (although they are). They are simply responding to the world around them. They hear stories of kids who go to zoos and meet a talking turtle and a waistcoat-wearing walrus. Their books dance with princesses, tigers, frogs, dragons, elephants, fairies, elves, cows, hobgoblins, horses, lizards, dinosaurs, butterflies, trees with doors, and bad-tempered ladybirds.

Of course they draw fantastic pictures of robots and wizards and fairies and monsters and cars and trains and the sun. They are in all their stories. You can buy fairy costumes, witches hats and princess dresses in a supermarket—and you can see a princess on the television. That princess is in REAL LIFE!

And Legoland is near London. All the buildings are made of TOY!

The elephant lives in India and Africa—it says so in that book. The lion lives in Africa and behind the wardrobe. You'll find it in those books.

It is not that there is no distinction between fact and fiction, reality and fantasy—it is all real fantastic fact. And the adults encourage this:

'You saw a fairy? *Really?* How lovely'.

'What a terrifying monster you've drawn—he's going to eat me up'.

'Have I told you the story about the wolf who eats Granny and dresses up in her nightgown and gets into her bed and pretends to the little girl that he really is Granny?'

Gradually, curiously, the child starts to quiz this. 'But fairies aren't *really* real, are they? I mean, not like *really here*, in this room?'

'Ok, I've got it. Elephants in Africa are *really* real. The lion behind the wardrobe is *story* real. I mean, I can go to Africa but I can't go to Narnia. That's right, isn't it?'

The child will feel some satisfaction in establishing such an insight. Knowing that it is toddlers and babies who try to eat a biscuit in a picture book. *It's only a picture, silly!*

The revelation may come in stages. The child eventually realizes that the Santa Claus in the shopping centre is just a guy dressed up. But he's a fake not because there is no Santa, but because *he's not the real Santa*.

This autodidact propels us onwards. Let's get to the heart of the matter. Let's nail it. Let's awaken ourselves to this division between real and imaginary.

And so our education progresses...

So our disenchantment progresses...

Re-enchantment is a slow reversal of this—and it can occur at any stage.

Re-enchantment is happily—if at times bewilderingly and frighteningly—sensing again that *Not-Quite-So-Sure* feeling.

Re-enchantment is happily realizing that you never lost that not-quite-so-sure feeling, and hence the lifelong allure of ghost stories, old dusty books in old dusty libraries, standing stones and woodlands at dusk...

Not-quite-so-sure about fairies.

Not-quite-so-sure about angels.

Not-quite-so-sure about ghosts.

Not-quite-so-sure about the visions in the drum.

Not-quite-so-sure about the spirit of the hillside.

Not-quite-so-sure about the friendship of a tree.

Not-quite-so-sure about the spirit of the hillside when there are plans to cut down the trees and build on the fields.

Not-quite-so-sure about the friendship of a tree when sensing that it might be cut down.

Not-quite-so-sure about something conscious in a woodland at night.

Not-quite-so-sure about so much more because being not-quite-so-sure makes the sense of not-quite-so-sure grow.

Re-enchantment is happily realizing that nobody has entirely lost that not-quite-so-sure feeling.

In fact, libraries, churches, homes and schools are bursting with stories of magic, fairies, angels, archangels, witches, princesses, goblins, strange powers, possessions, monsters, aliens...hauntings, healings, and hexings...ghosts, ghouls and ghoulies...Re-enchantment is happily realizing that you have to be quite odd not to have that not-quite-so-sure feeling. The world really is queerer than we *can* suppose.

This is what draws me to Borges. Long John Silver shares the bookshelf with Schopenhauer. Emily Dickinson sits quietly with Scheherazade. De Quincey and Coleridge drink wine with gauchos. Swedenborg reads the *Tao Te Ching* in Renaissance Florence. Beowulf and Walt Whitman dance a tango. Borges's bookshelves sing with *enchantment*.

In a 1926 essay called 'A History of Angels' he concludes with the following:

I always imagine angels at nightfall, in the dusk of a slum or a vacant lot, in that long, quiet moment when things are gradually left alone, with their backs to the sunset, and when colours are like memories or premonitions of other colours. We must not be too prodigal with our angels; they are the last divinities we harbour, and they might fly away.

I sense a gentle urging in his voice—don't be too quick to dismiss. Disenchantment can be sad.

*

I don't write fiction, I invent fact. (Borges)

In 'Feeling in Death' Borges felt that words suddenly made sense. Over the years, I have begun to understand, too, that words can make sense.

I customarily declare that Borges presents a world in which fact and fiction intertwine. I make much of this. But the knowledge only slowly took root. It is because fact and fiction *do* intertwine. Nothing is stable. We live mythically, poetically, comically, tragically. Our closest friends may be fictional. Hamlet, indeed, is soul-brother to many. Others know Don Quixote and Sancho better than they do their own friends. And our lives are fictional, perhaps with no author. Reality is immensely creative.

Don Quixote somehow intuited that, and from there we have those tremendous dialogues between Sancho and the Knight. Both dream each other whilst dreaming themselves. They were both dreamed by Cervantes, but Cervantes was also a dream of Don Quixote, who traipsed the Castilian plains imagining his author recounting his exploits. Borges wrote a poem about this, in which the Knight dreams of Cervantes losing his hand in the Battle of Lepanto.

IMAGINAL LANDSCAPES

Don Quixote knew Cervantes.

Don Quixote read *Don Quixote*. So he was right about his exploits being recorded.

As if to emphasize this, Borges elaborates tale after tale, poem after poem, essay after essay, in which the reader is confounded by the uncertain division between reality and fiction. Even his most outlandish stories (all his stories are outlandish) have Borges as character and narrator. Given that the 'Borges' of 'Feeling in Death' (an autobiographical account) is so similar to the 'Borges' of 'Tlön, Uqbar, Orbis Tertius' (a fiction)——are they the same? Did that conversation with Bioy Casares *really* take place? Which is the *real* Borges?

I have no idea, Borges would seem to answer, and to illustrate this he published a reflection called 'Borges and I', in which he struggles to separate one from another. The piece ends with the tremendous line 'I do not know which of us has written this page'. I might ask which Borges I keep mentioning here——the *real* Borges or the Borges I have imagined. There is no distinction, Borges-Borges would answer. Indeed the term 'Borgesian' evokes, precisely, this confusion between author, narrator, character and reader.

In another tale the old Borges narrator sits by a river and talks to a stranger, whom he quickly realizes is himself as a young man. Neither of them can determine who is dreaming who. The reader is no more able to determine. The reader, after all, is dreaming them both. Literature makes magic possible.

*

We have come into a world which is a living poem. Every thing is as I am. Bird and beast is not bird and beast, but emanation and effluvia of the minds and wills of men there present. Every one makes his own house and state.
(Emerson)

Swedenborg understood that for the spirit-minded man of science——Newton, Flamsteed, Linnaeus, Swedenborg himself——the natural world is the language of God. The stones, stars, planets, animals and oceans all reveal the mind of God. They are all magical systems. They may be read.

Literature too is a magical system and the fundamental text for Swedenborg was the Bible. Scrutinizing the Hebrew texts, he began to read the language of God and to develop his doctrine of correspondences.

This biblical exegesis is 'preposterous' and 'make-believe', huffs the author of Sherlock Holmes. 'Not thus does God send His truth into the world'.

Well, not thus did God send His truth into Conan Doyle's world, but thus into others'. Each system, each language, is magical to some, not to others. Everything is meaningful if there is the will to perceive meaning.

God's script was decipherable to Swedenborg in the Testaments. It was decipherable to Tzinacán in the spots of a jaguar. Jung perceived hidden divine language in archaic signs and codes, dream symbols and the hexagrams of the *I Ching*. Synchronicity is the sudden eruption of authorship. It is a dizzying moment of awareness that reality is infused with psyche. Borges sensed this, and described it in a concise answer in an interview:

> Perhaps coincidences are given to us that would involve the idea of a secret plan, no? Coincidences are given to us so that we may feel there is a pattern—that there is a pattern in life, that things mean something. Of course, there is a pattern in the sense that we have night and day, the four seasons, being born, living and dying, the stars and so on, but there may be a more subtle kind of pattern, no?

There are many magical systems that may guide the reader in the interpretation of this subtle pattern: herbs, music, trees, numbers, kabbalah, alchemy, astrology, philosophy, cards, crystals, saints... There are as many languages as there are explorers. None is the right one. None is the wrong one. They are all systems and they are all magical.

The more that you employ these systems, and the more you seek correlations between one system and another, the more you understand that the systems interact with reality—that they are reality. That is why they are magical.

The systems can be stretched to increase our understanding of the complexities of reality, or they can be bricked up to restrict enquiry. This, says Borges, is why we should be wary of becoming too faithful to any one system. Faith, Borges would argue, stifles imagination and creativity, as it encourages unquestioning support for one particular model of the universe.

Yet we are all shaped by the systems we inherit and inhabit. Dante, Swedenborg and Blake, in Borges's eyes, stretched the language of Christianity to its limits. They surpassed orthodoxy in their visions. This was their authenticity and their poetic beauty. Their faith fuelled their imagination, to the extent that they accommodated certain articles of their faith uneasily, heretically.

Literature demands imagination. The reader is encouraged to consider the reality of a fiction. Fiction animates imagination. The more it is stretched the more it becomes a means of engaging with reality—the more it becomes a mode of perception—the more creative it is.

This, to me, is important. We read a novel, and the narrative states 'that night Hector had a dream. He dreamt that. . .' Immediately, as critical readers educated in the art of hermeneutics, we are encouraged to seek meaning in this dream, and to anticipate its relationship to some event later in the novel. Why this dream? Why these features, these images? After all, if the dream is utterly meaningless why did the author choose to write it into the novel? It must be a clue.

We accept prophecies in literature. As such we know that Oedipus will murder his father. We do not argue with the Weird Sisters when they predict Macbeth's kingship. They are not cold guessing. They know.

Likewise we are trained to seek meaning in a character's name. Why is this fellow called Hector? What does the name Samuel Pickwick tell us about Samuel Pickwick the man? Why, we ask, is Humbert Humbert called Humbert Humbert?

We might consider Hardy's Wessex—Egdon Heath or Casterbridge—as characters.

Literature, you see, is *fantasy*. We are encouraged to seek such meaning only within its confines. Literature is permitted enchantment.

Beyond art. Ah—but no authorship, you see, so the meaning of a name is merely conferred, never intrinsic. Divination is nonsense. Dreams are not prophetic. The dead remain dead.

Re-enchantment is to permit meaning to creep back, to sense that meaning conferred *is* intrinsic; to understand that, like Don Quixote, our stories are written as they unfold.

Re-enchantment is thus making your life enchanting to an unknown reader.

Re-enchantment is being content with authorship without author.

Re-enchantment is understanding that dreams can be meaningful. Or not. Names can be meaningful. Or not. Divination is work with the future only by working with the present. The world is a magical system...

*

> *You know, Dante was wrong about hell, wrong about the meaning of that inscription on the gate of the Inferno in the first lines of Canto 3:* Lasciate ogni speranza, voi ch'entrate *(Abandon every hope, you who enter). Hell doesn't begin down there. There is no entry to the afterlife. Hell begins here, and here is where we should abandon all hope. Then we have the possibility, the hope, of some momentary happiness.* (Borges)

Heavens and hells are not hidden locations revealed at the point of death. They are here. They are states of the soul. They are consciousness. This was the gong that Swedenborg sounded for Borges. It sounded for me, too.

Borges often repeated the expression of George Bernard Shaw (which he assumed Shaw had learned from Swedenborg via Blake) that 'God is in the making'.

I love that. I see it as a compelling gnostic sentiment; God as an ideal of wholeness towards which the energy of our life propels us. Judgement is happening all the time. It need be no stern sentence, but a reassuring nod from within.

And so it is not where we go after death. It is here. It is who we are; and moving into death will not affect our true selves. Swedenborg's books are not answers to the question 'where do we go after death?' They are about realizing that we are already there—we simply move through a flimsy division of being or not being attached to a physical body. But even there it is quite unclear—as in *Heaven and Hell* the sensuous nature of the spiritual body appears to be intensified rather than jettisoned. Of course there is sensuousness, Swedenborg reminds us, why should there not be? Heaven is a state of the soul—it is where you are now.

And people do not suddenly change upon death—at least they change neither more nor less than they would in life, because life is life whether this or that side of death. Swedenborg saw some souls carrying books around, and consulting them when in dialogue. This is how it is. That is how they are. They are doing what they are doing, as everyone everywhere is. Nothing is permanent, and one soul may start giving his books away. Off on a different path now. *Heavenandhell* is now.

The moment of death is really not that important. The moment may alarm some, perhaps because death comes suddenly and unexpectedly. Perhaps they had never imagined being able to think about being dead once they were dead: 'My God, I'm dead and conscious!'

Yet that thought can happen at any stage: 'My God, I'm *alive* and conscious!'

Or it may not. Swedenborg paints some souls continuing in endless habitual spirals leading nowhere.

This is illustrated in *Arcana Caelestia* in a passage which Borges transcribes in two anthologies of fantastic literature, entitling the piece 'A Theologian in Death'.

The angels tell Swedenborg about the case of the early Protestant reformer Melanchthon. Upon dying Melanchthon is unable or unwilling to acknowledge that he is dead and continues with his theological treaties concerning faith as of greater value in heaven than charity. Over a period of time (though as Borges indicates elsewhere, there is no time in Swedenborg's heaven) he becomes entrenched in his dogmatic doctrine of faith, and distances himself ever more from divine love and wisdom. His pride and obstinacy eventually drive him to consort with sorcerers and demons. He excludes himself from heaven.

This passage demonstrates the severe critique—to the point of heresy—that Swedenborg maintained concerning doctrines of faith, perfectly encapsulated in a rich and damning statement in *Heaven and Hell*:

> This I can testify to, from all my experience of matters relating to heaven and hell; all those who professed faith alone in their doctrine, and in their lives were steeped in evil, are in hell.

After death, some people build up defences against understanding that their soul survives death. Just as before death defences are built. And it may take time to dismantle those defences through the magic of enchantment.

Swedenborg's hells are simply un-enchanting, populated by the disenchanted. And there is an enchantment to that, hence the thriving communities.

For others the transition into death is expected, as they understood that souls communicate regardless of their bodies; and once free of the body, what difference whether alive or dead? Of course the soul is alive, as it is communicating with other souls continually.

We attract and are attracted to communities of souls. One community may be hellish to some, heavenly to others. There are places and communities for everyone. They are not even hells and heavens, as that would imply cosmic order (I am not sure Swedenborg would agree with that). No up, down, left or right—just communities of kindred spirits. He writes in *Heaven and Hell*:

> Let me add to this that all people, even while they are still living in the body,

are, as regards their spirit, in company with spirits, although not knowing it. Through the spirits a good person is in an angelic community, a wicked person in a hellish one. After death as well the person enters that community. [...] A person is not actually seen as a spirit in that community while alive on earth, because at that time the person is thinking naturally. However, those who think in a manner abstracted from the body, because they are then in the spirit, sometimes are seen in their own community.

Swedenborg urged movement, activity, intrigue, imagination. Be flexible, recognize that nothing is fixed, heavens become hells become heavens—they are merely words. Blake reflected this in one of his provocative proverbs: 'he who binds to himself a joy, doth the winged life destroy'.

Why should there be any difference when you die in relation to who you attract, the activities you engage with? Rum, tobacco and sweets are often offered to the dead. Of course! People like rum, tobacco and sweets. No reason to give up tobacco simply because you are dead...

Are ancestors and angels attracted to the drum? Of course they are; those ancestors who like the drum. Some may not like the drum, and they may be attracted to another ritual environment. If in corporeal life they were drawn to one type of ceremony, it is likely that this appeal would not suddenly disappear. No reason to take up tobacco simply because you are dead...

Souls drawn to secret, solemn, sombre sanctuaries when embodied are probably drawn to such environments when disembodied. Souls drawn to political power, scheming and the adulation of lackeys may continue beyond death. 'Those who have found pleasure' writes Swedenborg in *Heaven and Hell*, 'in secretly plotting and being involved in underhand schemes are also found in those underground places, and they go into chambers so dark that they cannot even see each other, and they whisper in ears in corners. This is what the pleasure of *their* love turns into'.

Hence we should be cautious with our commerce with the dead. Not because they are dead, but because they were once living. We should be cautious with our commerce with the living.

This is most striking when considering Swedenborg's visions themselves. In keeping with his own accounts, we must assume that our experience of death will not resemble his, unless we have absorbed to a profound degree his particular landscapes so as to make them our own.

W B Yeats, for example, attributes a strong cultural influence upon Swedenborg's own appreciation of the angelic realm:

> Swedenborg because he belongs to an eighteenth century not yet touched by the romantic revival feels horror amid rocky uninhabited places, and so believes that the evil are in such places while the good are amid smooth grass and garden walks and the clear sunlight of Claude Lorraine.

This is a beautiful image—Swedenborg's heavens populated with periwigged gentlemen strolling in lofty discourse through manicured gardens, tapping their polished walking sticks against the gravel path.

So did Swedenborg's Viking ancestor chiefs require the funerary boats and treasures with which they were buried? Of course, as this was their cultural cosmology. Did mummification aid the souls of the departed Pharaohs? Of course, for this was what they prepared for. A burial at sea is appropriate for a sailor. Falling in battle was appropriate for Borges's ancestors on the frontiers of the early Argentine republic.

'But no one is condemned', writes Borges. 'Each searches for the company and companions of his choosing, and he searches according to the appetite that has dominated his life'.

Why should it be otherwise? Anyone who has spent their lives in 'a world of conspiracy and sordid politics' is unlikely suddenly to seek the company of angels upon dying.

Or not. Maybe they have changed their tastes and interests. Why not? All is change.

Borges wrote a story that seems to illustrate this. In 'Dead Men's Dialogue' two dead soldier-statesmen from the early Argentine Republic, Rosas and Quiroga, return to Buenos Aires. (Rosas returns from his grave in Southampton, England). Faceless and ghoulish souls flock around them, amidst an atmosphere of squalor and putrescence. Rosas is still Rosas—proud, defiant, power hungry and authoritarian. Quiroga, whom he had had murdered, seems wiser in death, keener to move on, grow, develop. Quiroga explains to Rosas that nothing can persist forever, not even in death, and that even as they speak, 'Just look, we are both changing already'. Rosas responds 'It must be that I am not made to be a dead man'.

The mutilated crowd remains in the battle-scarred landscape in which they died. Rosas is thus still their general (or enemy). This was the landscape and company of Rosas during his life—and so it continues in death. The tale then concludes with the equally mysterious commentary of the anonymous narrator: 'They spoke no more, for at that moment Someone called them'. This Someone who calls them is perhaps Borges, or perhaps the reader, drawing them away from that hellish terrain of hatred. To let go of blame, of hatred and of guilt, is to raise the anchor of the past and allow onward passage.

In an earlier poem entitled 'Rosas', Borges reflects on the power the living can have over the dead:

Even God has forgotten him,
and to delay his eternal extinction
for a pittance of hatred
is to turn our contempt into charity now.

To maintain hatred for Rosas is to maintain Rosas as Rosas. In the poem, Borges seems eager to release his ancestral hatred of Rosas, so as to free himself from the burden of hating, and to free Rosas from the burden of being hated. Both Borges and Rosas will now be free to move.

In another of Borges's tiny tales, called 'The Legend', Cain and Abel meet again in some distant desert, and each has forgotten who slew who. Guilt and blame have been jettisoned. The brothers are unburdened:

'Was it you that killed me, or did I kill you?' Abel answered. 'I don't remember anymore; here we are, together, like before'.

'Now I know that you have truly forgiven me', Cain said, 'because forgetting is forgiving. I, too, will try to forget'.

In another tiny tale, Borges reminisces with a friend about the night they may have committed suicide:

A: (now deep in mysticism) Quite frankly, I don't remember whether we committed suicide that night or not.

There is a beautiful sense in these fragments that life moves on. Whether before or after death, there is no compulsion to bind fast to an event or feeling. Souls are free to let go of the past. To forget is clearly a deeper cleansing than to forgive, which implies blame.

In interviews as an old man, Borges stressed his wish to die and cease being Borges. An eternity of being Borges horrified him. There is no contradiction that this sentiment should accompany a deep respect for vision of Swedenborg's life after life. Why maintain this withering physical form and this bagful of memories, he seems to be saying. Let go and travel freer, 'for it would be frightening to know that I am going to continue, frightening to think that I am going to go on being Borges. I am tired of myself, of my name, and of my fame, and I want to free myself from all that'.

We are in communication with angels and with the dead now. We are reading Swedenborg, Emerson, James or Borges, engaging, dialoguing, imagining, projecting, surmising. Communication between souls is not always through the lips. It is here. We are already there. It is not about recognizing the survival of the soul *after* death, but the survival of the soul *now*.

Swedenborg was thus not an explorer of distant shores—inner, outer, up, down, transcendent, beyond time and space... He was an explorer of this world—our world—this time, this moment.

*

Among the Dakota Sioux, Haokah used the wind as sticks to beat the thunder drum. (Borges)

This was a profound moment of understanding for me. I can illustrate with an example.

Drumming recently in a small group we hit a beautiful rhythm. I moved away in my mind, pursuing a path down a tunnel—moving away. Further, deeper, away. The groove was sustaining. Energy for a lengthy journey. I began to look out for spirit guides—perhaps Swedenborg's angels, perhaps the bird I have encountered before. Yet something of Swedenborg came before my vision. Whom do you seek? Helpers? Guides? Open your eyes, my friend. If you seek allies, be receptive to their presence. I was drumming with friends, a powerful, magnificent rhythm. Come out of the tunnel. Come back to the present. Here are spirit helpers.

Of course. I was in a community of spirits—my fellow drummers—splendidly embodied. So be with them. Seek their help, their advice, their strength, their guidance. Ask it of them. Feel it coming from them. And there it is! What tremendous strength—drumming with friends—with ensouled beings. Creating together an astonishing pace and place. Explore it. Explore it with them. They are your allies. Go with them.

So, I tried to hold onto the other drummers—to hold onto their drumming—yet also to move along this tunnel. Together on a soul journey. They have come to the drums seeking strength, peace, guidance, healing—or seeking nothing more than the drums.

I understood that I, too, was a spirit helper, drumming with others, moving somewhere together.

Can I say that? Can I say that I am a spirit helper? Why not! My friends have appeared in my dreams. I have appeared in my friends' dreams. I have tried to soothe someone who was hurt. I have tried to summon healing energy for myself and others. I have drummed with others. Is our engagement simply physical, material? My sense is that we interact with others far beyond the limitations of our personalities and our bodies. We are vessels filled with consciousness. Yet consciousness is not limited by the vessel. We communicate through dreams and drums as much as through hugs and handshakes.

There is a threshold to cross, as I see it. It consists of feeling that our capacities exceed the vessel, that some mode of consciousness pertaining to us as individuals is not restricted by space, and perhaps not restricted by time. Cross that threshold and a vast panorama of possibility opens up. Jung captured this perfectly:

> There are these peculiar faculties of the psyche, that it isn't entirely confined to space and time. You can have dreams or visions of the future, you can see around corners, and such things.

A monster is more real if more meaningful. Less real if less meaningful. And the monster may be fully material (a soldier who tortures or the medic who supervises) or devoid of materiality (Sauron, for example). What is important is the meaning invested in the monster's power.

Indeed this is a strategy of survival. A shaman meets a monster in the lower world and pulls an uglier face than it. Deny its power over you. Form an alliance with it rather than cower before it in fear. Max, the hero of Maurice Sendak's *Where the Wild Things Are* does precisely this. He dresses as a wolf, acts wildly and is banished. He journeys across time to the land of the wild things:

> And when he came to the place where the wild things are, they roared their terrible roars and gnashed their terrible teeth and rolled their terrible eyes and showed their terrible claws till Max said, 'BE STILL!' and tamed them with the magic trick of staring into all their yellow eyes without blinking once. And they were frightened and called him the most wild thing of all and made him king of all wild things.

Max's power over the monsters is such that he can sit on their shoulders and dance the Wild Rumpus—the most empowering dance I can imagine...

I sense this illustrated in Borges's *Book of Imaginary Beings* with regard to the many beasties in whom we no longer believe. They are no longer meaningful, and thus merely constitute a historical curiosity. They are certainly not frightening, unless we are frightened by them. In which case they resume their meaningfulness and their monstrosity.

A monster that is not monstrous is not a monster.

Hating Rosas continues to make Rosas hateable. Hating Rosas keeps Rosas Rosas.

Cain and Abel are trapped by the monsters Guilt and Blame until they forget who murdered who.

Don't feed the beast. He'll grow.

Numina only have the power that we invest in them, which is the power that they invest in us. If the god is vengeful and terrifying, it is because there is a part of us that needs vengeance and fear—a part of us that is vengeful and terrifying.

Two three-year-old girls ate the cake and tasted the dram of sloe gin offered to a figurine of a saint. Immediate reflection shows that to be a delightful rather than a transgressive course of events. This is not the space for solemnity. Would the saint mind that two little girls took her offering? How could she? She's a saint!

With such a thought, I have come to renegotiate my view of the Conquistadors, colonists and slavers of the New World, and their evocation of Christ prior to acts of extreme savagery. Whilst they may have preached Christ the Redeemer to communities they took to be needful of redemption, deep inside they were appealing to Christ to redeem their own cruel hearts. Only a healer of such power could forgive the horribleness of their acts.

*

We believe in the lion as reality and symbol; we believe in the Minotaur as symbol but no longer as reality. (Borges)

Every investment of consciousness gives form. We have learnt to separate the lion of the savannah from the lion of Narnia. We do not expect to find the Minotaur in the Hampton Court Labyrinth or the Longleat Maze.

But are some imaginary beings more real than others? Swedenborg's angels, for example, share the pages of *Book of Imaginary Beings* with the Eloi and Morlocks of H G Wells.

I was initially perturbed by this, and tried to unravel some hierarchy or taxonomy of daimonic beings. Borges—what's it going to be? You say that Swedenborg's journeys are authentic, but you place his angels next to obvious fictional characters. Swedenborg was no novelist, you insist, he was an explorer. Yet Wells invented his future beings. You said that Dante was no mystic because he invented his poetic cycle, so are his angels less real than Swedenborg's angels?

Ultimately, I understood that my questions were failing to encompass the creative spirit of the imagination.

Hamlet is no less real than Oliver Cromwell. Cromwell was *materially* real, whereas Hamlet is a fictional—albeit astonishingly significant—creation. I have not seen the bones of Cromwell. I have seen Hamlet, about eight times in different settings, on the stage and on the screen. I have seen Ophelia die many times.

I feel that the question is not so much about materiality, but about autonomous consciousness.

There is something reportedly so astonishingly real and consensual in people's experiences with the serpent of ayahuasca visions or elves of DMT-induced visions that there is a fascinating debate about their ontological status. How real are they? Well, they are immensely real—as people have experienced them, and described them, and spoken with them (more like have been *spoken to* by them).

Yet for others they may be nonsense—pure make-believe.

They are both real *and* make-believe and neither real *nor* make-believe.

Are they real or are they make-believe? YES!

That is no problem. The lion of the savannah is real and make-believe. After all, I am not touching him as I write this. He is as make-believe as the Minotaur.

The question that fuels the debate about DMT elves is not their materiality but the sense that their lives carry on when they are not being observed.

That is to say, we imagine a horse continuing to be a horse even when we are not observing the horse. We do not imagine that the horse requires our observation in order to exist.

This is the sense Swedenborg presents with his angels. He meets them, greets them, talks with them, then leaves them. They have jobs to do regardless of Swedenborg's presence.

Many have reported with DMT or ayahuasca experiences that they appear to interrupt activities already taking place; that they have stumbled into an elven engagement rather than created it.

This is a compelling question, I feel, especially when presented with accounts of astonishingly real entities.

Jung was troubled by this. Whilst, as visible in his essay on UFOs, Jung was ever cautious about speculating on the material nature of psychoid entities—a speculation that might lead to the suggestion that ghosts, apparitions and daimons may be somehow beyond the psyche—nevertheless, as is clear from the complex text of *The Red Book*, he was deeply concerned about the possibility that the spirits who visited him were something more than aspects of his unconscious; that they were autonomous, ontologically distinct beings.

When in dialogue with Elijah and Salome, Jung declares: 'I can hardly reckon you as being part of my soul [...] Therefore I must separate you and Salome from my soul and place you among the daimons'. Such is the autonomous nature of Salome and Elijah that when Jung confronts them and suggests that 'You are the symbol of the most extreme contradiction', Elijah retorts: 'We are real and not symbols'.

Later, Elijah returns to this matter and explains: 'You may call us symbols for the same reason that you can also call your fellow men symbols, if you wish to. But we are just as real as your fellow men. You invalidate nothing and solve nothing by calling us symbols'.

Elijah's response is astonishing, as he urges Jung to understand that we are all daimonic beings, forever encountered symbolically by others, forever encountering others symbolically.

Not everything in *The Red Book* is as clear as this response, and I feel its impact lies with Jung's bafflement when confronted with figures of such overwhelming autonomy. Hence his ultimate desire to tell them that they are not real because he is dreaming them. His guru figure, Philemon is—by Jung's own account—far more of an individuated soul than he is. He is, indeed, a wise old man.

Jung clearly understood in his dealings with Philemon, Salome and Elijah—so dazzlingly illustrated in *The Red Book*—that there is something utterly beyond our consciousness that is nevertheless part of our consciousness. He learns to feel that they are real *because* he dreams them.

Borges, I sense, would add 'You're dreaming me—I am real!'

In this sense Jung moved from asking whether he had dreamt of his dead father or whether his father visited him in his dreams, to concerning himself with what his father had to say.

The question of autonomy, as such, like the question of materiality, fails to address the full scope of the imagination. The dream is the location of encounter. Both Jung and his father participated in the dream encounter. Like Borges as an old man talking on a bench with Borges the young man, both are dreaming each other.

What does a dead relative have to say? What are these elves saying? What do we seek with them and they with us? Listen to the voices, do not pathologize them. Curiously, this is a well-reported feature of ayahuasca encounters: don't be so astonished by us, say the elves, the serpent, the jaguar or the luminous woman, listen to what we have to say...

*

Demons are nothing other than intruders from the unconscious, spontaneous irruptions of the unconscious complexes into the continuity of the conscious process. (Jung)

My intuition leads me to concur with Jung that the beings, the daimons, the angels and monsters, are all aspects of our greater self, which is beyond our individual self. They are both within and without, as the psyche is not limited to a designated extension.

In this respect the entities are not so much created by the imagination as encountered through the imagination. The encounter is the result of a creative process which gives form and context to a formless force. In this respect the daimonic beings do operate autonomously and consciously, but the location of encounter is the creative imagination. They are figures of the unconscious insofar as it is through the deeper strata of the unconscious that they may be encountered.

But so we encounter ourselves and each other through the deeper strata of the unconscious. Deeper resonance between souls—perhaps established through love, compassion, communication—permits our engagement with each other, with the world, on a daimonic basis. This is enchantment—allowing symbols to be symbols, souls to be souls, myth to be myth...

Consciousness gives form to consciousness. Consciousness participates in consciousness.

As Sartre depicted so poignantly and yet so bleakly, we give form to each other and to ourselves. We invest in each other, shaping, moulding, forming the contours of self, personality and body. We do not and cannot exist in a vacuum devoid of other modes of consciousness, otherwise there would be no interaction, no flow, no communication, no consciousness itself.

There may also be a denial of consciousness, and in this case tortuous regimes of the past and present deny the fluid selfhood in another. You are ONLY a prisoner/captive/detainee. You are scum, vermin—subhuman. This seems like draining someone of consciousness. This is the tragic backdrop of modern conflicts. This is Sartre's *L'enfer*. Garcin, in Sartre's play *Huis clos*, will be a coward for eternity in hell, unless he and his two companions can forget his cowardice and allow him to move on. Which they won't. Perhaps *we* should forget his cowardice. Let me say it—Garcin is not a coward! Move on, my friend...

This is the geography of Swedenborg's hells. The angry man becomes anger. The guilty man becomes guilt. They become imprisoned.

This is the geography of our world. The cruel man becomes cruelty. The murderer is murder.

I envisage consciousness flowing into form and both giving form and being shaped by form. And whilst that form may or may not be material, it is the form, and not the material, that interacts and communicates with other modalities of form-defined consciousness. Thus a friend, who by day is mostly defined by his physical form, has often appeared to me in night-visions as a bear. He need have no awareness of this. I, more than he, give him bearness.

Shamans may shape-shift. Witches were persecuted for taking animal form, and their animal familiars were hurled into the same flames for assuming human intelligence. Scientists are still desperate to prove or disprove that one twin may suffer the pain of the other twin across great distances. Why the mystery? Neither twin is bound by their physical form in a specific location. Their consciousness is more entangled than most.

A reflection on this matter is often considered taboo. It raises eyebrows. Is laboratory proof really necessary as evidence? What does our experience imply? Is there anything transgressive about this—that we are more than the vessels that carry us?

I pondered deeply over this in the company of a chestnut tree. Does this tree have consciousness in and of itself? Well probably not, but then, do I? Can I conceive of individual human consciousness devoid other human consciousness? My conscious form is a continual process of interaction with others. Without investing in others how would I invest in myself? We give form to others and are given form by others. Consciousness is participation. Thus the more I invest in this tree, talk to it, listen to it, sing to it, meditate with it, the more the tree invests in me, talking to me, singing with me, meditating with me. I am evoking tree consciousness now as I write.

It seems to me not a matter of faith, nor credulous New Ageism, to recognize that our sense of self and our sense of others are a perpetual ebb and flow of consciousness.

Kant was critical of Swedenborg in *Dreams of a Spirit-Seer*, but it becomes clear that Kant fully accepted the spirit world. Only he, like Russell, felt that knowledge of it was so personal and non-consensual that it could not constitute workable, reliable data pertinent to Enlightenment discourse. Thus Swedenborg's ethical dimension—drawn from biblical hermeneutics and conversations with angels—was inconsistent with truth claims about knowledge. It was opinion, not fact.

And so the spirit world is simply another way of describing *this* world populated by consciousness manifesting in physical or non-physical forms. *We* are spirit and *we* exist. By naming Kant, by invoking him, I give spirit—conscious—form to him, although my knowledge of Kant is scant, and thus my investment in Kant is scant.

We invest consciousness in all aspects of reality—in memories, animals, trees, dolls, talismans, landscapes, dream figures, rivers, and the dancing flames of a campfire. We are expected to grow out of investing consciousness in a doll. Yet we still do communicate with dolls, if only to keep a child happy, which is to keep us happy, which is to keep the doll happy...

It seems easy for us to deny tree consciousness, and hence the readiness to fell them.

I find that Robin Hood becomes ever more meaningful to me. Outlaw, wood-bound, a spirit of the trees.

And so for Borges the phoenix and the centaur were outdated beings of the past, evoking little investment today, as were the 'horde of monsters (tritons, hippogriffs, chimeras, sea serpents, unicorns, devils, dragons, werewolves, cyclopes, fauns, basilisks, demigods, leviathans, and a legion of others)'. Even the dragon had been impoverished by bad art:

> Time has notably worn away the Dragon's prestige. [...] The Dragon is perhaps the best known but also the least fortunate of the fantastic animals. It seems childish to us and usually spoils the stories in which it appears. It is worth remembering, however, that we are dealing with a modern prejudice, due perhaps to a surfeit of Dragons in fairy tales.

The angel, however, retained some of its ancient allure and thus sang to Borges, imploring his investment, his protection. Just as 'God is in the making' so are angels in the making (but perhaps not dragons).

I have paid little attention until writing this to the descriptions of DMT elves, but I have invested tremendously in the Moomins. They are thus more real, as they are more meaningful. Part of me longs to be Snufkin, the contented wanderer, yet part of me recognizes myself in Moomintroll, the cautious worrier. As the years pass, I sympathize ever more with Moominpappa's refusal to be disenchanted. I, along with countless other readers, invest the Moomins with life, as they invest in us.

This was beautifully illustrated in a conversation with one of the same three-year-olds who had pilfered the saint's cake. On another occasion she was scared of something.

'Don't worry', I said. 'La Santina is watching over you'.

'No! *I'm* watching over La Santina!'

Of course!

Swedenborg invested in Borges, providing guidance, inspiration, reassurance. Borges invested in Swedenborg, discussing his works, painting his landscapes, praising his adventurous Viking nature. Borges has invested in me, captivating then taunting me, writing in riddles, yet urging me ever onward in pursuit of enchantment.

Snufkin wanders south in the winter, with his flute, tobacco and pipe, and returns to Moominvalley when the winter snow is melted. Mythic lives are played out in literature. Spring is blossoming as I write this. Snufkin will be back soon, I hope.

*

> *I have proposed the Latin* mundus imaginalis *for it, because we are obliged to avoid any confusion between what is here the* object *of imaginative or imaginant perception and what we ordinarily call the* imaginary. *This is so, because the current attitude is to oppose the real to the imaginary as though to the unreal, the utopian, as it is to confuse symbol with allegory, to confuse the exegesis of the spiritual sense* with an allegorical interpretation. (Henry Corbin)

This book's title borrows a term first expressed by Corbin as a means of articulating the subtle world of experience of the imagination—the *Imaginal*. This is the liminal land of enchantment that bridges the material and the psychic. It is, as James Hillman merrily described, the expression of the heart and of the soul. It is the landscape populated by gods, monsters and daimons.

'As Corbin goes on to say', writes Hillman, 'we believe these figures are subjectively real when we mean *imaginally* real: the illusion that we made them up, own them, that they are part of us, phantasms. Or, we believe these figures are externally real when we mean *essentially* real—the illusions of parapsychology and hallucinations. We confuse imaginal with subjective and internal, and we mistake essential for external and objective'.

Whenever I attempt to explain the term I feel that I fail, as its fluid essence spills from our language. The imaginal relates to a dismantling of the hard division between an external material reality and an internal psychic landscape. I will try to express it through illustration.

On my first experience of journeying to the lower world in a shamanic ceremony, I gazed at tumultuous images behind my closed eyes for the duration of the drum rhythm. When later describing the images, I was underwhelmed, recounting that I had merely imagined a tunnel, leading down, and I had merely floated in and out of the tunnel, and I had seen a kind of door, which I had opened, and I had seen some sort of animal, and so on. But I had simply made it up. It was no vision—it was just random thoughts.

Precisely!—came the response from the circle-holder—that is precisely what the experience is. It is the imagination.

I have come to understand the strength of this response, and I have recognized how an articulation of the perceptive power of the imagination is at the heart of the language of mysticism, of religious and magical practice, of the numinous and of enchantment. The psyche, as Jung experienced and described, is far less constricted by the limitations of matter than we are educated to believe. Hence the imagination is capable—especially with training—of ferrying consciousness and extending our perception, far beyond our expected limitations. Hence the shamanic vision is not *simply* fantasy—it is a mode of perception imbued with the limitless scope of fantasy.

'This faculty', writes Corbin in the opening chapter of *Swedenborg and Esoteric Islam*, 'is the imaginative power, the one we must avoid confusing with the imagination that modern man identifies with "fantasy" and that, according to Sohravardi, produces only the "imaginary."'

Yet there is a sombre and solemn tone to Corbin that deters me from using the term imaginal too playfully. Corbin stressed movement towards the angelic, towards perfection. Darkness and its attendant monsters do not appear to be welcome in his vision of the imaginal. There is something rather too clean about Corbin, which leaves my example of the visions of the drum slightly ill-formed and chaotic. I sense that Corbin would baulk at such muddy tunnels, leaf litter, wood pigeons and foxes. He might say that I was cavorting with the djinn.

I find greater welcome within the worlds of Jung and Hillman. There is an animistic, pagan quality to my experiences that finds accommodation in their vast embrace. Hillman, I feel, would join me cavorting with the djinn.

My most resonant experiences of what may be called the imaginal are woodland-bound, dark and damp and mossy. Fallen trunks from which new growth sprouts. I enter the woodland on foot and in reverie. I follow the swirl of bark and the spread of branches, entering treeness. Hands plunging deep deep into the rich clammy mulch. This is where Tree and I meet—an imaginal space both material and soulful.

My woodland is thus real and imaginary, mapped and fantastic, true and false.

It is a fiction. It is a fact. It grows in the landscape and the inscape. It is both matter and psyche.

And yet so educated are we in this division between matter and psyche that we accommodate only very reluctantly any indication that they may become intertwined in this imaginal landscape of dreams, fantasy and desire.

Above all, the imaginal is the meaningfulness of art and the resonance of myth.

In this sense, I concerned myself with two astonishing accounts from Borges, keen to establish whether they were real or fictional.

> Haydée Lange and I were conversing in a restaurant in the centre of town. All of a sudden, I remembered that Haydée Lange had died a long time ago. She was a ghost and didn't know it. I felt no fear, but felt it would not be right, and perhaps rude, to reveal to her that she was a ghost, a lovely ghost.

This magical small piece made me question whether he had really engaged in a conversation with the dead Haydée or whether he had simply imagined it for the purpose of a fiction. Then it struck me so clearly: it is the same thing. A dream encounter is a dream encounter. The imaginal is the creative power of the imagination.

Likewise Borges wrote: 'Asleep, in my dreams, I see or converse with the dead. None of these things surprises me in the least'. Did this suggest that he was a medium, able to contact the dead? Of course! Why not? He has written that he has. He dreams of the dead and communicates with them. We dream of Borges and imagine his dreams. We interact in the imaginal.

Mediumship is communication with spirits. We are all spirits. We communicate. We are all, in a sense, mediums.

It is not only the dead who haunt.

*

There is something in the dragon's image that appeals to the human imagination, and so we find the dragon in quite distinct places and times. It is, so to speak, a necessary monster, not an ephemeral or accidental one, such as the three-headed chimera or catoblepas. (Borges)

IMAGINAL LANDSCAPES

Consciousness congresses around meaningful forms. Joseph Campbell, nourished on Jung, would describe these forms as the archetypes of the hero's journey. They are essential character matrices encountered in dreams, myths, tales, novels, poetry, theatre, film—which is to say, in our lives. They are meaningful as they are germane to people, events, episodes and landscapes of our lives. They are, as Borges suggests, necessary monsters. They sing to our imagination.

The character of the first card of the Major Arcana of the Tarot, *Le Mat* (The Fool) is off, briskly, energetically and rashly, on his or her quest. He or she may be the hero, everyman, each of us. She may receive magical help or learn magic from *Le Bateleur* (magician). She may be guided or rebuked (the same thing) by religious or secular (the same thing) authority. Her fortunes will soar and plummet. She may have her world turned upside down and be hung by her ankle. She will no doubt encounter death. She will be tricked or helped (the same thing) by the wily devil. And so on.

She may meet old greybeard the hermit, indeed she may meet him in one of his many avatars as Merlin, Gandalf, Obi-Wan or Dumbledore. The Tarot is simply a story—it is as magical as we choose to make it.

Research into mysticism is in some way a mystical adventure. Reflecting on the hero's journey is setting out on that very journey. Engagement with Jung's term *individuation* can activate the very meaningful quality of the term.

Borges recognized the heroic nature of Swedenborg—valiant Viking!

I have identified the dynamic of the hero's journey in Borges's tales. In 'The South' a very Borges-like character lives out his heroic destiny whilst, perhaps, never leaving hospital. He dies, guided by a toothless old gaucho, under the open sky in a ritual of compensation for his studious and inactive life.

'The Ethnographer', ultimately, is an account of a powerful shamanic initiation.

In one of his final tales, called 'The Rose of Paracelsus', a naïve novice calls on Paracelsus and asks him to perform a miracle. Paracelsus declines and the novice, humbled, leaves. Paracelsus, alone and weary, then performs the miracle.

And so it goes on. Tale after tale, poem after poem, in which a character forges ahead on a journey of discovery, entering deeper into consciousness, seeking meaning where meaning is never forthcoming.

*

> *Reality has no need of other realities to bolster it. There are no divinities hidden in the trees, nor any elusive thing-in-itself behind appearances, nor a mythological self that orders our actions. Life is truthful appearance. The senses do not deceive, it is the mind that deceives, said Goethe.* (Borges)

And yet one need not live in a world brimming with conscious forms. The grass does not scream when you mow the lawn. Chairs, desks, fences, gadgets, wisteria bowers and mushrooms need not be alive, as one risks rocking reality and provoking psychic seasickness.

Just as we would risk our integrity and our sanity were we to love unconditionally every commuter on the rush-hour train, so we require for our mental well being material solidity. We need inert matter.

An over-enchanted world could be monstrous, overwhelming.

This is what is pathetic about Don Quixote in Book Two. The giants, princesses, fiends and sorcerers that he conjured up in Book One have now been taken up by his companions—and he with them. He cannot extricate himself from this pantomime without ceasing to be who he now is. His monsters are now truly monstrous.

Erik Lönnrot, the detective of Borges's tale 'Death and the Compass', is so steadfast in his magical system that he can be controlled by his enemy, and drawn deeper into the very fiction that he created and which kills him. Neither Lönnrot nor Don Quixote ever clap their hands, like Alice, and say 'You're nothing but a pack of cards!'

I often talk to a drum before playing it. I thank it for being a drum and for letting me play it. But I need not. It's just a drum. Play it. That's thanks enough.

That same three-year-old child might break the figurine of the saint. Don't worry. It's only a model. The saint is not broken.

A treasured piece of jewellery that once belonged to an ancestor gets lost. Don't worry. It was only a thing. And now it's gone.

Seeing one magpie is no indication that things will go wrong; it is an invitation to think about things going right.

Clocks tick, kettles boil, people live and die, and a cigar is just a cigar.

A perpetual state of exultation would soon cease to be exultant.

Despite the desires of inspectors in Britain's schools today, no teacher can be outstanding all the time. If they were, they would not be outstanding.

Perpetual ecstasy would not be ecstatic.

Perpetual rapture would not be rapturous.

*

Being an agnostic means all things are possible, even God, even the Holy Trinity. This world is so strange that anything may happen, or may not happen. Being an agnostic makes me live in a larger, a more fantastic kind of world, almost uncanny. It makes me more tolerant. (Borges)

Borges emphasized that agnosticism led not to despair but to rapt wonder at the mysteries inherent in the universe; indeed there is scarcely an interview in English (of which there are many) in which Borges does not express his 'amazement', 'bafflement', 'wonder' and 'puzzlement' confronted with these mysteries. He also repeatedly located the English word 'maze' within 'amazement', and consequently perceived the motivation for his lifelong employment of the maze or labyrinth in his art. 'Mazes are to be explained by the fact that I live in a wonderful world. I mean, I am baffled all the time by things. I am astonished at things'.

Like Emerson, he returned again and again to the dialogue between faith and intellect in Swedenborg. Never allow faith to quell the spirit of enquiry. Intelligence is a divine gift allowing man deeper engagement in the mysteries of the world. 'To the requirement of righteousness, Swedenborg adds another, never before mentioned by any theologian: intelligence'.

This seems to me important, and it is central to the whole of Borges's engagement with his readers. Enquiry is an act of salvation. Faith alone is not sufficient—one must enquire and experience. One must not abandon intellect.

The reader of Borges's fiction is invited to solve the riddles of the tales. The reader is mystified by what is fiction and what is real. The reader is thus encouraged to solve the riddles of reality. All is real. All is fictional. All is baffling.

Borges paid particular attention to an episode in Swedenborg's *Heaven and Hell* in which a hermit, who had renounced everything in life, found himself unfit for heaven. Having abandoned his critical faculty—his intelligence—he was unable to converse with the angels and unable to appreciate divine love. A solution is reached in which he is granted an eternal desert in which to continue his impoverished existence in death.

This is an ethical matter, as salvation does not arise through the grace of God, nor is hell a punishment. In Swedenborg's vision we are free to choose our own worlds. Borges illustrates this:

> Whether we believe in the immortality of the soul or not, we must recognize that the doctrine revealed by Swedenborg is more moral and reasonable than one that postulates a mysterious gift gotten, almost by chance, at the eleventh hour. To begin with, it leads us to the practice of virtue in our lives.

To abandon intellectual engagement is to reject our own intrinsic curiosity and to favour doctrine over experience. It is to squander our most precious talent, to renounce a divine gift.

Be critical, be awake, do not be foolish and credulous, Borges urges us. Do not be too convinced about anything. The more convinced, the less flexible to accommodate new and different visions of the world. Explore the philosophical, metaphysical, religious or political system being offered. Does it stand up to scrutiny? Does it correlate with other systems in other landscapes and other timescales? But once entering a system, never abandon the spirit of enquiry by making the assumption that this system is now the great language of reality. No, it is one of many languages. It is one of many magical systems. As such, the deep exploration of philosophical systems inevitably creates a critical distance that allows for conflicting or even contradictory systems not to compete but to combine and enrich the tapestry of epistemologies.

So if we can trust no one system, what value can we place anywhere? If reality really is not so stable, then how does one learn to discern between one system and another? Where *can* one place faith?

I meditated on this matter, imagining—conjuring—responses from Borges. The Borges in my imagination responded thus:

What can we know, you ask me. I have no idea. Tell me your story— your explanation—and I'll hear you out with as much sympathy and respect as I've heard out the stories of Plato, Schopenhauer, Emerson, the Arabian Nights, Kabbalists, alchemists and mystics. They are all as beautiful, imaginative and plausible as each other...

Yet not all systems are equal. Not at all. Some systems are atrocious. Nazism was. It idealized the Fatherland, privileged the myth of Aryanism, and debased the Germans by insisting that the Germans debased others. It encouraged violent stupidity; and only the stupid cling slavishly to a political—which is mythical—ideology.

Nationalism in general is awful. Peronism was a tawdry spectacle—a cheap pantomime. Most political systems are fairly ugly—I don't think revolution really occurs unless it is poetic. I have never seen any political revolution that isn't ultimately bad taste, merely a new set of clothing on the same corruption and brutality. And it will always be thus, because politics is power.

Religious systems, also, can be ugly, mean-spirited and mealy-mouthed. Argentine Catholicism, as far as I'm concerned, propagates the ludicrous doctrines of heavenly reward and hellish punishment, whilst showing no concern with the mystery of death or the astonishing claims of the mystics. All one learns is how to pray louder than the screams of prisoners.

Some magical systems are not really magical—just entertaining. Use your intellect—enter the system and try to unravel it. If it collapses, then abandon it and go deeper into ones that speak of mystery. Don't simply subscribe to a new newspaper.

There are systems that merely reinforce the models of reality that you have been taught at school, university and at work, and as such the rich complexity of reality is painted over.

Look for the calligraphy that vibrates with magic.

Look for the traditions that have angered the inquisitors and made respectable burghers hide indoors.

What magic do they deal with?

That stern and driven William Blake, for example—what on earth was he trying to say? Stevenson's pirates—are they not splendid? That miserable Schopenhauer—did he not poetically sacrifice himself to redeem us poor humans from being bewildered, lost and frightened? Does he not wail for us? And Nietzsche—did he not go mad with rage and energy so that we may not? Sufi poetry—are there any metaphors anywhere else so exquisite? Quevedo and Joyce—they prised loose the mosaic tiles of language and rearranged them in such ingenious ways to *create such extraordinary worlds. Whitman—what force, what vigour, what power of prairie song in his heart. He urges us to be strong and carefree but always aware of our companions on the road. Take that companion by the hand and sing as you tramp the dusty highway.*

Buddhism is the perfect system that is no system, simply a state of meditative consciousness—the Buddha is neither man nor god but a possibility within us. Buddhahood like Christhood is a state of the soul.

Swedenborg—Swedenborg... he talked with the angels and instructed us how to live richer, fuller and more inspired lives. He teaches us not to wait for heaven, but to inhabit it now, to seek angelic guidance here, now, in this world. Hells are not punishments; they are states of the soul, and we are free to enter or leave such hells. All is movement. All is flux. Think. Explore. Contemplate divine love and heavenly wisdom. Never abandon the intellect—in fact, energize the intellect with the fuel of curiosity, poetry, love and intuition.

So be aware—not every system is equally viable of exploration...

Thus spake the Borges of my imagination, who is really me, a projection of my reflections upon a historical figure. A part of my consciousness.

*

Everyone who says I am a mystic is just an idiot. (Jung)

Perhaps I am being cagey in using the word *consciousness* instead of *spirit* or *soul*, as the word *consciousness* has an aura of respectability. Were I to replace the words, it might imply that I had abandoned reason and rational enquiry, that I was declaring an article of flimsy faith.

Bertrand Russell encouraged the use of dialectic dialogue in order to work through an argument and to loosen one's ties to a particular perspective:

> I have sometimes been led actually to change my mind as a result of this kind of imaginary dialogue, and, short of this, I have frequently found myself growing less dogmatic and cocksure through realizing the possible reasonableness of a hypothetical opponent.

Following his advice, I have imagined the critical voice of Russell himself as a hypothetical opponent responding to my writing. Would he scoff at my suggestions about consciousness, communities of souls, death, angels, enchantment? Have I uttered untruths?

Russell exhorts us to seek only what is true, and not to place our faith in matters (like, for example, Christianity) simply because they provide solace or comfort or are determined by tradition. This is all very well, but I cannot help thinking that Russell's position was influenced more than most by his knowledge of mathematics. 'Mathematics', Russell argued, 'rightly viewed, possesses not only truth, but supreme beauty—a beauty cold and austere, like that of sculpture'.

I would be happy to place my faith in what is true, but I find it difficult to determine what is or is not true. Indeed the question becomes circular. Russell advises against holding fast to any philosophical, religious or political system. 'In all affairs it's a healthy thing now and then to hang a question mark on the things you have long taken for granted'. Yet, as I see it, recognizing and understanding Truth is itself a position requiring a certain faith in this discovered Truth.

Thus any statement about truth is by its own definition not true. Including this statement. This is an ancient paradox.

Despite insisting as an agnostic that if evidence for something is not forthcoming then one should 'withhold judgement', Russell rejected notions of life after death as 'nonsense'. I prefer to follow his initial advice and suspend judgement. In so doing, like Borges, I am enraptured by numerous contrasting and at times conflicting theories about soul, spirit and matter and the survival of some spark of consciousness after death.

Is this nonsense? This is the dilemma we find ourselves in when considering the many metaphysical questions thrown up by Swedenborg. Clearly it is not all *lies*. So what then? Swedenborg was clearly not alone in recognizing the awesome scope of the soul, and its subtle ties to the body.

In fact, in my limited survey of cultures and traditions across the world and across time, it would seem that only our modern industrial 'Western' culture lionizes the position that consciousness is limited to brain activity, and thus the cessation of the brain constitutes the cessation of consciousness. Is it not 'nonsense' to declare so forthrightly that the soul's survival of death is 'nonsense'? To see death as absolute oblivion is itself a matter of faith.

I prefer to suspend judgement, which allows astonishing possibilities. Yet by reserving judgement I am nevertheless wary about claims proposed.

This is a situation I find amply illustrated by Jung, as also by Borges. Jung never missed the opportunity to remind his readers that 'I am an empiricist, who keeps within the boundaries set for him by the theory of knowledge'. It was this spirit of enquiry that urged him onwards into an examination of the power of symbols, images, dreams, visions, alchemical interactions between *physis* and *psyche*. Despite his immense sympathy with systems that beget a sense of the numinous, Jung insisted that he was a *doctor* and not a *magus*. Consequently, he wrote in a ponderous and at times impenetrable style, arguing every point from multiple angles, citing hundreds of examples from arcane texts for each statement, proving by his dazzling intellect that he was not placing his credulity in any system that demanded simple faith.

Jung was likewise adamant that he was no mystic. I sense in Jung's refusal to be called a mystic a declaration that he, like Swedenborg, was not a madman nor a charlatan. He was emphasizing his healthy spirit of critical enquiry.

Borges, meanwhile, maintained the same degree of critical distance with mysticism as he did with philosophy:

> Many people have thought of me as a thinker, as a philosopher, or even as a mystic. [...] People think that I've committed myself to idealism, to solipsism, or to doctrines of the cabala, because I've used them in my tales. But really I was only trying to see what could be done with them.

Borges's refusal to be called a mystic reveals, I feel, a similar sentiment. I imagine him saying: 'Do not call me mad or—worse still—credulous or naïve because I am fascinated in the strange margins of human experience. All my exploration is fuel for my fiction'.

This is a strikingly Swedenborgian sentiment. Even in heaven—especially in heaven—Swedenborg urges his reader to be alert, engaged, curious. The hermit squanders his intellect and cannot engage in metaphysical debate with the angels. Melanchthon blinds himself through declarations of faith and ends up preferring the company of spectral ghouls. Borges reminds us of this: 'Swedenborg imagines heaven, above all, as a series of theological conversations between angels. And if a man cannot follow these conversations he is unworthy'.

I construe this pattern in a Borges poem called 'Ajedrez' (chess). Twin sonnets seem to form the two sides of the chessboard. The animated pieces do not know that they move at the will of the chess players. Yet the players do not know the hand of God, controlling their moves. Yet God does not know of the hand of yet another god, controlling His moves, and so on.

In bleaker moments I have imagined this poem as a depiction of angelic existential angst. A person questions life's purpose. When he dies he approaches an angel saying, 'Now that I'm dead, can you tell me what it is all about?' The angel answers, 'Damned if I know. I've been troubled by the same questions. Why am I an angel? Let's go ask God'. So they go to God, who answers, 'Damned if I know. Let's go ask...' and so on. The chess match continues. 'Este juego es infinito', says the poet, 'this game is infinite'.

Both Jung and Borges lowered rope ladders deep into the cave of oddity, and lit the lamps of their respective endeavours (psychology and literature) to guide them through theses dark and dripping chambers. At any stage they could scramble back into daylight, having placed their faith in no particular theological or metaphysical system. This is the interface between faith and experience.

It might seem, for example, that I have placed my faith in claims about the extent of our consciousness and the persistence of the soul after death. But my position is that this is the most reasonable position to take. Our experiences, stories, poems and myths are alive with such realities. Testimonies abound, across time and culture. The argument against any of these myriad testimonies, however, is always the same: it is merely psychological.

If, however, we permit within the 'merely psychological' the dimension of the imaginal; and if we accommodate a greater understanding of the interpenetration of consciousness in matter, then, as I argue above, a threshold is crossed in which vast possibilities are engendered. This is how Borges defines agnosticism. It is a state of mind not in which everything is possible, but in which nothing is impossible as a matter of principle, 'even God, even the Holy Trinity. This world is so strange that anything may happen, or may not happen'. We should be neither naysayers nor proselytes.

*

Borges is our Virgil; only he knows the way.
(Alastair Reid—poet and translator of Borges)

Borges spoke often about the poetic power of *The Divine Comedy*, and he exhorted his readers to read Dante. There is a passage of *Inferno* that he wrote about with great sympathy. It is when Dante arrives at the *nobile castello* where his guide Virgil—as a pagan—will remain.

But Virgil is essentially a sad figure who knows he is forever condemned to that castle filled with the absence of God. Dante, however, will be permitted to see God; he will be permitted to understand the universe.

Borges detected in Dante a deep love and respect for Virgil. Although Dante will be saved, and will ascend towards the godhead, he is enthralled by the noble company of these damned souls. Dante perhaps harbours a certain envy for Virgil. I sense that Borges felt Dante, and not Virgil, to be the truly sad one. Sad because he cannot rest in the noble castle, but must proceed towards perfection.

Borges is our Virgil. He leads the reader through the most astonishing mythic landscapes. We descend with him into the hells of frontier warfare and military politics of nineteenth-century Argentina. We meet the ghosts of Rosas and Quiroga, surrounded by hordes of mutilated dead. He recounts the exploits of Erik the Red and describes for us the martial halls of Valhalla. He introduces us to Plato and Plato's teacher, Socrates. We are dazzled by the monsters and shape-shifters of Ovid and Apuleius. He reads to us about the song of Bede's Cædmon and he recounts Stevenson's relationship with the Brownies. He sings to us of celestial dragons, underground goblins, fairies, elves, pixies, hippogriffs and the Banshee. He gives voice to Asterion, the Minotaur, who longs for Theseus to redeem him. We meet desert djinn, Aztec gods, Zoroaster, Christ and the Buddha. He guides us through Blake's complex mythologies. Borges leads us through the hellish swamps and the celestial paradise of Swedenborg's *Heaven and Hell*.

And yet, like Virgil, he cannot lead us to the divine. That is for the faithful and Borges, I imagine, would be happier to remain with the reader in the pagan castle, engaging in merry dialogue with Homer and Heraclitus, Orpheus and Ovid, Lucan, Horace, Hippocrates, Avicenna, Galen, Averroes and Virgil, than rising towards the heavenly rose.

But what of Swedenborg?

Borges made so much of Swedenborg's heterodoxy. Brought up a Lutheran, Borges reminds us, Swedenborg rejected the idea of salvation through God's grace alone. Swedenborg also was unable to accommodate the essential article of faith of the Trinity. Doctrine contrasted with his experience, and so he rejected doctrine. And this, Borges continues, is the great and wonderful heresy of Swedenborg. Brave Viking as he was, he had no fear in upsetting orthodoxy.

I sense that Borges would secretly expect to find Swedenborg strolling along a gallery of the *nobile castello*, grinding lenses with Spinoza, observing Jupiter's moons with Galileo, and discussing alchemy with Newton.

Here, indeed, be giants.